JUNIOR CERTIFI

LESS STRESS MORE SUCCESS

English Revision

Higher Level

Larry Cotter

Gill & Macmillan

Gill & Macmillan

Hume Avenue

Park West

Dublin 12

with associated companies throughout the world

www.gillmacmillan.ie

© Larry Cotter 2011

978 07171 46 78 9

Design by Liz White Designs

Print origination by O'K Graphic Design, Dublin

The paper used in this book is made from the wood pulp of managed forests. For every tree felled, at least one tree is planted, thereby renewing natural resources.

For permission to reproduce photographs, the author and publisher gratefully acknowledge the following:

© Alamy: 3, 23, 39, 44, 49, 72C, 82, 123, 133; © BBC Photo Library: 139; © Bridgeman: 116; © Corbis: 12, 60, 94; © Deanne Fitzmaurice / Ricardo Romagosa: 61; © Getty Images: 7, 56, 64, 108, 110, 113, 119, 137; © Imagefile: 106, 109; © Inpho: 67T, 68; © Press Association: 67B; © Picture Desk / Kobal: 84, 148; © Rex Features: 46, 48, 77, 88, 98; © Topfoto: 102; Courtesy of EMI Music: 75; Courtesy of Iarnród Éireann: 73; Courtesy of McDonalds: 72L; Courtesy of NASA: 41; Courtesy of Nike: 72R; Courtesy of Nissan Ireland: 69; Courtesy of Penguin: 51; Courtesy of Random House: 126; Courtesy of RTÉ: 79, 80; Courtesy of Twitter: 66; Courtesy of Walker Books: 144; Courtesy of The Washington Informer: 74.

The authors and publisher have made every effort to trace all copyright holders, but if any has been inadvertently overlooked we would be pleased to make the necessary arrangement at the first opportunity.

CONTENTS

Introduction

This book will guide you through your revision for Junior Certificate Higher Level English. Each chapter deals with a section of the exam and ends with sample questions from previous exam papers. As part of your revision, it is important that you familiarise yourself with the **structure** of the exam:

Exam paper breakdown

Paper 1

Paper 1 takes 2 hours and 30 minutes.
You must attempt all four sections: Reading, Personal Writing, Functional Writing and Media Studies.

Recommended time	Section	Marks available
30 minutes	Reading	40 marks
60 minutes	Personal Writing	70 marks
30 minutes	Functional Writing	30 marks
30 minutes	Media Studies	40 marks

Paper 2

Paper 2 takes 2 hours and 30 minutes.
You must attempt all three sections: Drama, Poetry and Fiction.

Recommended time	Section	Marks available
25 minutes	Drama Q1 Unseen	30 marks
25 minutes	Drama Q2 Unseen	30 marks
25 minutes	Poetry Q1 Unseen	30 marks
25 minutes	Poetry Q2 Studied	30 marks
25 minutes	Fiction Q1 Unseen	30 marks
25 minutes	Fiction Q2 Unseen	30 marks

How to use this book

Read each chapter carefully. You will notice a grid at the beginning of each chapter. **Use this grid to record important information about your revision for the exam.** Record each of the following:

- The date you first **read** the chapter.
- The date you **revised** it.
- The date of your final **recap**.

This process will ensure that you cover all sections thoroughly. You can use the information in the grids to keep an eye on your **overall progress** in revising for the exam. Your completed grids should look like this:

Read	Revised	Recapped
10 December	14 March	3 June

You should also pay close attention to the **aims** in each chapter. These highlight the **key skills** you need to develop as you work through the book.

You will learn how to approach all sections of Paper 1 and Paper 2. Be aware of the **key points** and **exam focus** reminders throughout the book. They will help you to focus on the most important aspects of your revision.

There are many **sample questions** in the book. Use the **helpful hints** and **sample answers** to learn how best to approach each question. By practising sample questions in the book, you will improve your ability to answer well.

At the end of each chapter, **real exam questions from past papers** are provided. They are a really useful guide in understanding the structure and style of Junior Certificate Higher Level English exams.

Paper I

1 Reading

Read	Revised	Recapped

- To read in a **focused** way.
- To build skills of **comprehension**.
- To **support answers** with suitable quotations.
- To give clear **explanations**.

The first section of Junior Certificate English Paper 1 is entitled Reading. This section will test your abilities in:

- **Reading.**
- **Understanding.**
- **Writing.**

The comprehension passage is usually non-fiction and the topic covered will set the tone for the rest of the paper. For this reason, you should **always approach the Reading question first**. There may be certain ideas or feelings discussed in the comprehension passage that could provide a title for the Personal Writing question later on. Obviously, the composition titles will make more sense to you once you have read and answered the questions on the comprehension passage.

The **key skills** for writing a good comprehension answer are:

- **Focusing** on the question.
- **Quoting** in support of your answer.
- **Explaining** in your own words.

Three relevant points are sufficient for high marks. Ensure that each point is clearly explained and well supported by examples from the passage.

You should always pay attention to the **number of marks** being awarded for each part of the Reading question. It is important to **divide your time** on the basis of the **marks available** for each answer. Usually four questions will be asked and all four parts are awarded equal marks.

In the past, examiners have been critical of students who could not write more than a few lines in the Reading question. You must **develop** and **sustain** your answers, usually over two or three paragraphs.

The first question will probably focus on **factual details** in the passage. Later questions require greater **analysis** and **explanation** from you. The last question is usually about the writer's **style**. This means that you must discuss his or her **language** and explain **why you think they chose the words** and phrases used in the passage.

There are **40 marks** for the Reading question and you are instructed to spend **30 minutes** on this section. **Do not spend more time** than this on the Reading question, or you may run out of time for the rest of the paper.

How to approach the reading question

1. Spend **30 minutes** on the Reading question.
2. **Read the passage** and use a coloured pen to **highlight key words** or phrases as you read.
3. **Read the questions** carefully once again **marking the key words** in each question.
4. **Think carefully** about exactly **what it is you are being asked**.

What follows is a series of sample Reading questions, some from previous Junior Certificate papers. Attempt as many of these questions as possible, in order to practise for your exam. Look carefully at any sample answers given.

A   Read the extract below and answer the questions that follow.

Darling, Don't Do That
Tim Dowling

By normal decent standards, young children are hideously disgusting. It takes discipline to suppress the feelings of revulsion that their personal habits provoke.

> As a parent, you must learn that no matter what state your children are in, you still have to pick them up, kiss them and hold their grubby little hands. You must love them unconditionally, even when they're sick on you. Even when they give you lice.

The author shows his reaction to his children's lack of cleanliness. His introduction is striking because it is full of expressions of **horror.**

On the whole, children under the age of six prefer to be sticky.

> They just don't feel right leaving the house without an all over coating of yoghurt, juice, jam, chocolate or another substance.

You can tell that little children enjoy being filthy by the fuss they kick up whenever you try to make them clean. Nothing fills them with horror like the sight of a soapy J-Cloth.

And why shouldn't they enjoy messiness? They live in a world where walking around with a lollipop in your hair doesn't necessarily put you at a social disadvantage. Other children never seem to mind that their companions are so grubby.

The awful thing is that their filthiness rubs off on you – literally. My own standards of what constitutes a clean shirt have dropped alarmingly. Being flecked with someone else's breakfast is now my normal state. I no longer shudder when my boys wipe their **bogies** on my jumper. I consider it progress that they're wiping their noses at all.

Of course, the real no-go area is the place they call their own – the back seat of the car. This raisin-studded, rubbish-strewn hellhole is generally not worth cleaning. The seat belts are stiff with grime, the seats are damp and the door wells are tightly packed with half-eaten apples, old sweets and crisp dust.

Perhaps the most irritating thing about children is that they combine their love of filth with an irrational squeamishness.

'I can't eat this chicken,' one of mine will say. 'It's touching spinach.' Yet I have seen this same son eat cat food!

Likewise my three-year-old will not allow anyone to handle his precious bedside collection of old bananas. Even rearranging them slightly brings howls of disapproval. I tend to look on the bright side, and hope that this daintiness will one day develop into a sense of personal hygiene. In the meantime, I'm not holding my breath. Neither am I holding my nose.

Detailed images help the reader to picture the scene.

Colloquial phrases (the language of everyday speech) remind us that Dowling is writing about small children.

Examples of children's unusual attitudes to food.

Questions

1. How does Dowling prove that children enjoy being dirty?   (10 marks)
   *Look at the key words in this question. You must **find evidence** that children like being filthy.*

2. Describe the tone of this piece.   (10 marks)
   *Tone is always an expression of **feeling** or **emotion**. Look for 'feeling' words in the passage to discover the tone.*

3. Comment on the author's use of imagery and colloquial language. (10 marks)
   *You must **give an opinion** about the **images** and **language**. Do they help to make the article interesting? How?*

4. How does the use of humour add to this article?   (10 marks)
   *This is a **leading question**. In effect, the answer is **strongly suggested** by the words used in the question itself. To answer this well, you need to **explain** the **comical effect** of the writer's style.*

SAMPLE ANSWERS

ANSWER 1

Dowling gives several examples of children who seem not to mind being dirty. He tells us how his own children often have a 'coating of yoghurt, juice, jam' or 'chocolate'. This is evidence of a fondness for being 'sticky' rather than being clean. Dowling's children do not object to this stickiness in themselves or others but they do hate being cleaned. According to the writer nothing can fill 'them with horror like the sight of a soapy J-Cloth'. When he tries to wash them the 'fuss they kick up' shows how they would prefer to remain dirty.

> **Key quotes** are evidence from the passage, used to support a point.

On the other hand they don't seem to object to the condition of the back car seat they frequent. This place is a 'rubbish-strewn hellhole'. Dowling leaves us in no doubt that a great deal of discarded dirt litters their back seat.

All of Dowling's evidence is drawn from experiences with his own children. He assumes that since his children are 'hideous', then all other children are the same.

ANSWER 2

The passage begins with a tone of revulsion. Dowling says young children are 'hideously disgusting'. The article is full of revolting images, for example 'the seat belts are stiff with grime'. This man seems to be shocked that children can be filthy in so many ways.

Later on, he expresses his acceptance of the fact that his children are dirty and that this affects his own hygiene. When he says that being 'flecked with someone else's breakfast is now my normal state', we sense that Dowling is resigned to his fate as the contaminated Dad of such mucky children. He has come to terms with the fact that his boys wipe their 'bogies' on his jumper. His outrage and horror has been replaced with humorous submission and he cheerfully admits that he now considers it 'progress that they're wiping their noses at all'. We begin to wonder if he was ever truly upset.

Ultimately there is a tone of pride and affection for his children. The writer still believes that he must love his children 'unconditionally'. Even though he lists their foul behaviour he admits that he still picks them up, kisses them and holds their 'grubby' little hands.

> Key words in the answer identify the feelings or **tone** of the author, e.g. 'shocked', 'cheerfully', 'pride', etc.

ANSWER 3

The images in the article appeal to our senses. Dowling gives us several hideous pictures to consider; my favourite is of his children wiping their 'bogies' on his jumper. He uses three adjectives to describe the back seat of the car as a 'raisin-studded, rubbish-strewn hellhole'. The visual effect is clear and disgusting.

There are also many images appealing to our sense of touch. When he says you must love your kids 'even when they give you lice' my scalp begins to itch immediately. Another feeling is the sensation evoked by 'half-eaten apples, old sweets and crisp dust' in the door well of the car. This image manages to conjure up both the touch of these discarded foods and the awful mixture of smells I associate with them.

He uses colloquial language because he is, after all, describing children. Instead of mucus they wipe 'bogies', their dirty hands are 'grubby' and the car seat is a 'no-go area'. More formal vocabulary would be unsuitable and far less funny!

> **Colloquial** language is informal and close to the style of everyday speech.

ANSWER 4

The writer includes several examples of humour in this article. He seems to be making a serious point about how important it is to always love your children, until he says 'even when they're sick on you' and 'give you lice'. These comical examples change the mood instantly. Most of the comedy arises from the way he describes the behaviour of the children.

One example is 'how walking around with a lollipop in your hair' doesn't bother other children. The idea of children behaving like this is humorous to me. It's also funny when he tells us about the child who refused to eat a healthy meal of chicken because it was touching spinach, but bizarrely the same child had been known to eat cat food.

Without the humour, this article would be a fairly routine complaint about the hygiene of modern children. The fact that Dowling makes light of his family's behaviour and is even willing to ridicule his own appearance helps us to see that the consequences are not really serious. The idea of children being filled with horror at 'the sight of a soapy J-Cloth' is amusing and enjoyable.

B   **Read the extract below and answer the questions that follow.**

Take **30 minutes** to do this Reading question and make sure to **use the steps** outlined at the beginning of this chapter to help you write high-quality answers. Notice how each question carries **equal marks**. **Divide your time** into four equal periods in order to get a high grade.

A Swim for the Soul

Róisín Ingle

If Brian hadn't come back from Bombay for Peter and Aoife's wedding I would never have known what it was like to swim with a dolphin. Brian, known variously as Yoga Boy or Siddhartha to his friends, is the kind of brother who comes rushing over to your apartment and says: 'Oh my god, man, guess what, there is a dolphin swimming in the exact place on the west coast where you nearly drowned. We are totally going to swim with that dolphin. Biba says it has healing powers, man. It's meant to be. We have got to check it out.'

For reasons entirely to do with Brian's arrival in the Western world, my resistance was already low and I knew that trying to change his mind on this one would be pointless. The same week he had more or less frog-marched me to the East Wall Community Centre where I was introduced to his newly invented form of yoga. I'll be the first to admit those three days of Soma yoga were an edifying experience, both for body and mind, but after a few too many Downward Dogs (don't ask) this yoga novice felt dog rough. And I just didn't have the energy to argue.

So I meekly accepted the fact that on the first Sunday in October, we were going to be driven by another yoga teacher, Biba, to Fanore in County Clare, where Dusty the dolphin has been delighting observers since she legged it here from her previous hang-out at Doolin.

'That Fungi in Dingle is a bit of a tart,' said Brian, who overnight had meta-morphosed from a yoga teaching osteopath into an expert on the personalities of seafaring animals. 'Dusty is the alternative dolphin.'

Apparently that Kerrymaid ad ('a dolphin is a man's best friend, ha, ha, ha, ha') hasn't done poor Fungi's reputation much good. Some non-believers say Fungi probably expects royalty cheques and appearance fees, while newcomer Dusty is like one of the freshly plucked contestants on *Popstars: The Rivals* and hasn't become jaded by all the attention.

The night before the day trip, some family skeletons had been dragged out of the cupboard by Brian and there were lots of tears before bedtime. I had been acting as a sort of mediator during Brian's trip home. We were emotionally hung over as we left Dublin. Dusty, named after Dusty Springfield, who had her ashes scattered in the Atlantic, represented the cure.

As Brian had pointed out, I nearly drowned at Fanore in the early 1980s in the days when being bashed about by twenty-foot waves was my idea of fun. I was ten years old and I remember thinking: 'This is it, this is the end.' It was dark and we really shouldn't have been swimming at all, Damien and me.

He was a family friend, a father figure really, whom I loved. When I finally reached the shore, I looked back into the sea and he was gone. I hadn't been back since. He was buried in Fanore, just a few minutes away from where Dusty lives now.

We found his grave and I realised for the first time that he was only thirty-four when he drowned. I walked out to the spot where it happened. There is a sign there now: *Bathing is Unsafe in this Area.* Better late than never, I suppose.

We saw the caravan where we waited all night to see if he might come back and make us a cup of tea and laugh so hard his curly black hair would shake. I closed my eyes and imagined him waving from his blue Renault 4. I was so glad I had come.

After that, and a break for what we prayed were dolphin-friendly tuna sandwiches, we were ready to meet Dusty. Brian and Biba wore matching wetsuits. I wore my swimming togs and, inexplicably, a black Prince Naseem T-shirt.

The cove was crowded with boys in canoes and people in boats and children paddling among the rocks. Every few minutes we would hold our breaths as the dolphin flipped out of the water, sometimes far away and sometimes so close you could reach out and touch her.

There was something magical about all these people who had just come to spend time with or to observe such a magnificent wild creature. Even swimming in the Atlantic Ocean, for the first time since the last time, was an incredible experience. I don't know if it was Dusty or the fact that I was returning to a special place I had tried to forget about for too long.

Anyway, as corny as it sounds, I felt at peace bobbing around in the seaweed, the sun shining down as Dusty seduced us all. And I thanked her as I got out of the water. For drawing me back there, for reminding me of the good times. Tired, depressed, emotionally hung over? You could do worse than head west for some dolphin-therapy. Like my brother says, it's healing. Man.

Questions

1. What kind of person is Brian Ingle? (10 marks)

2. Do you think Róisín Ingle has a good relationship with her brother? Explain your answer. (10 marks)

3. This is a very dramatic piece of writing. What makes it so dramatic? (10 marks)

4. Would you like to visit Fanore after reading Róisín's article? (10 marks)

C   **The following Reading question is taken from the 2004 exam.
Read the passage and answer the questions that follow.**

'Call the usher! The pleasure of movie-going is becoming a pain, thanks to noisy, guzzling, mobile-phone-using talkers, kickers and general pests.' So said Hugh Linehan in an article in The Irish Times. *The article appears here in edited form.*

Shhhhhhhhh!

Maybe it's because I'm a spoiled snobbish elitist – and that's not something I'm happy about – but I have to confess I'm finding it increasingly painful to go to the movies with the rest of you, the great paying public. It's not because of the cinemas – standards of projection, sound, seating and ventilation have improved out of all recognition over the last ten years – but (and I am sorry to say this) your standards of behaviour seem to be disimproving all the time.

Kickers are a real source of irritation. The kicker problem is exacerbated by the design of modern cinema seats – a kicked seat reverberates right along the row, so that it can be nigh-well impossible to figure out where it's coming from. In the 1970s, they called this Sensurround and people paid to experience it in movies such as *Earthquake* and *Towering Inferno*. Nowadays, you can have your own personal towering inferno as you reach boiling point after two hours of bone-shaking juddering.

Up until recently, the mobile phenomenon seemed to be spinning out of control. Cinemas were buzzing like beehives with the wretched things and some buffoons even had the cheek to strike up conversations on them during the film. There will always be buffoons, but a corner seems to have been turned in recent times. Thankfully, cinemas have now taken to putting reminders on the screen telling people to switch off their phones, and many appear to be doing so. On an electronically related topic, by the way, what sort of benighted fool needs a watch that beeps on the hour, every hour?

I have some sympathy for those who feel nauseated by the smell of warm buttery popcorn which is so much a part of the multiplex experience, but it doesn't bother me that much. If people want to eat wildly overpriced, grease-saturated cardboard, then that's their business. At least popcorn has the virtue of being (almost) silent food – far better than the high-pitched crackle of the jumbo crisp packet or the extended kitchen-sink gurgle of the almost-drained Coke.

To my mind the real problem in cinemas these days is talkers. They're everywhere and they come in a variety of species. One kind can't help giving a blow-by-blow commentary on the movie. They're bad enough, but there is worse. Top of the list come those who just utterly ignore the film in favour of their own chat. Western society has devised countless places where people can communicate with each other, but cafes, restaurants or street corners are just not good enough for these people – apparently not when they can have the added pleasure of spoiling other people's enjoyment.

Then, there are those who think that any break in the dialogue has been inserted by the filmmaker expressly for them to start talking. The minute there is a pause of more than a couple of seconds they launch into conversation. This is not to forget the downright stupid, who spend most of the time asking questions: 'Who's she? What happened there?' By the time they've got an answer they've missed the next plot point, and the whole weary rigmarole starts all over again.

What is the reason for this plague? The general decline in politeness in society may have something to do with it, but it doesn't fully explain the seemingly unstoppable desire to talk when the lights go down. We don't want funereal silence; a good comedy, horror or action movie can be immeasurably improved by the communal experience of seeing it with an audience. People can shriek or laugh to their hearts' content, and there is a real sense of a shared magical experience. After all, we're all together in the cinema ... in the dark. And you never know who is sitting next to you!

(2004, Paper 1, Section 1, Reading)

Questions

1. Hugh Linehan outlines a number of complaints about cinemagoers' behaviour. List two examples of behaviour he finds particularly irritating. Basing your answer on the text, explain why he finds these examples irritating. (10 marks)

   *There are two parts to this question: **list** and **explain**. Make sure to complete both parts of the task.*

2. Hugh Linehan describes himself as a 'spoiled, snobbish elitist' in the opening line of the passage. Based on what you have read, would you agree with this description? Support your answer with reference to the text.   (15 marks)

   *You are free to agree or disagree, but this is another **leading question**, where the answer is suggested strongly in the wording of the question itself. To score full marks here, you need to **supply evidence** that the writer is 'spoiled' or expresses 'snobbish' views. Then you must **explain why** the words quoted are 'snobbish' or 'elitist'.*

3. Basing your answer on the way the passage is written, how serious do you think the writer is in his criticism of the behaviour of cinema audiences? (15 marks)

   *The final question is usually a style question. In order to score well here, you must focus on **how** Linehan expressed his views through the language and imagery used.*

SAMPLE ANSWERS

ANSWER 1

Hugh Linehan is annoyed by the behaviour of people who eat in the cinema. He is distracted by the 'high-pitched crackle of the jumbo crisp packet', which prevents him from hearing the film clearly. A similar interruption is caused by Coke drinkers and the 'extended kitchen-sink gurgle of the almost drained' cans. Both types of offender disturb him because the food they consume is noisy, unlike the relatively harmless popcorn eaters who choose 'silent food' instead.

While Linehan rails against the noise caused by eating, he reserves his most bitter venom for a group he labels the 'talkers'. They include people who offer 'a blow-by-blow commentary' on the action of the film, threatening to spoil it for other viewers. Worse still are the audience members who carry on a conversation, oblivious to the film.

He also finds that a species of viewer will wait for a 'break in the dialogue' to talk. The worst are the 'downright stupid' interrogative talkers who irritate by asking countless questions.

What all these villains have in common is a tendency to create unnecessary noise, which makes it more difficult for a serious viewer to hear what is happening in the film.

> This answer **lists** two types of complaint (noisy eaters and talkers) and **explains** what precisely the writer objects to ('tendency to create unnecessary noise').

ANSWER 2

I agree that Hugh Linehan comes across in this passage as being a 'spoiled, snobbish elitist'. His argument against a whole range of people is based on the premise that he alone should determine acceptable behaviour for the cinema. He objects to those who kick, use mobile phones, eat or talk as if they were interrupting a private viewing organised solely for his personal pleasure.

When he points out that 'you never know who is sitting next to you' he appears to forget that the cinema is a public performance for which audience members pay an entrance fee. Once I pay to see a movie and comply with the rules of the Cineplex, then I am entitled to enjoy the film like all other paying customers.

If Linehan's restrictions were enforced, there would be far fewer people in the cinema. 'Buffoons', 'benighted' fools and the 'downright stupid' currently pose a problem for him; and by excluding them, he would appear to favour an audience composed entirely of curmudgeonly bores who take films too seriously.

> Pick out the **main idea** or premise of the writer's argument.

> Then the **logical consequences** of this idea are discussed.

Answer 3

I do not think Hugh Linehan should be taken seriously. He exaggerates a slight problem and suggests that it has reached epidemic proportions and become a 'plague'. One instance of this hyperbole is when he compares the shake caused by a person kicking a row of seats to a simulated earthquake.

Hyperbole is obvious exaggeration for the sake of emphasis.

The list of complaints is entirely trivial and the level of behaviour does not constitute a serious 'decline in politeness'. If he were genuinely suggesting barring unsociable behaviour in the cinema then I think he would give examples of truly offensive or rude conduct. Eating crisps and talking are minor complaints and most of us put up with them as a matter of course.

I think the writer is merely letting off steam rather than proposing a serious change in cinema admission policy!

This is a clear and confident **personal response**, well supported by quotation.

D **The following Reading question is taken from the 2009 exam. Read the passage and answer the questions that follow.**

In the following edited extract (from Singing for Mrs Pettigrew: A Storymaker's Journey*) the award-winning writer Michael Morpurgo talks about the 'creative fusion' behind his writing and explains how he goes about his craft.*

1. I have often wondered in four decades of writing how it is that time and again my stories seem to gather themselves, write themselves almost (the best ones really seem to), cover the empty pages almost effortlessly – once I get going, that is. Each one is, I believe, the result of forces of a creative fusion, a fusion that simply can't happen unless certain elements are in place, a fusion I don't properly understand, but can only guess at. But it is an informed guess.

2. At the core of it is the life I have lived: as a child in London, as a son and a brother on the Essex coast, away at boarding school, then as a soldier, a student, a husband, a father, a teacher, farmer, traveller, lecturer, storyteller, grandfather. I didn't live this life in order to write stories, of course – for at least half of my life I had no idea I

even wanted to write – but without its joys and its pain, its highs and its lows, I would have precious little to write about and probably no desire to write anyway.

3. For me, memory is the source material that is needed for creative fusion – the memory of falling off a bike into a ditch; of collecting shells on a beach near Zennor; of running away from boarding school; of loving the paintings of Cezanne, the music of Mozart and the poetry of Ted Hughes; of a single lark rising into the blue. So it is no accident that every one of these things has made its way later into a story of mine.

4. But memories themselves are not enough to create the fusion that fires a story. To read widely and deeply, to have soaked oneself in the words and ideas of other writers, to have seen what is possible and wonderful, to have listened to the music of their words and to have read the work of the masters must be a help for any writer discovering his own technique, her own voice.

5. My own writing has taken years to develop – it is still developing, I hope – and it has happened in parallel with my life and my reading. Once the spark is there, then comes the time for research, and with research a growing confidence that I have the wherewithal to write it and then a conviction that I have a burning need to write it.

6. But I must wait for the moment before I begin, until the story is ripe. This process can be five minutes (unlikely) or five years. All I know is that you can't hurry it. The story will be written when the moment is right. I learnt some time ago not to force the pace, not to dictate the story but to allow the story time to find its own voice to weave itself, to dream itself out in my head so that, by the time I set pen to paper, I feel I am living inside that story. I must know the places; I must know the people. I may still not know exactly what will happen – and certainly how it might end. That often emerges through the writing. But I do know by now the world of my story intimately, its tone and tune and rhythm. I feel like I am living inside it, that even as I am writing about it I am not the creator of it at all, but simply telling it as it happens, as I witness it. And when it is written, I read it over, to hear the music of it in my head, to be sure the tune and the story are in harmony. No note must jar, or the dream of the story is interrupted.

    The last and most important element in the magic that produces this creative fusion is the sheer love of doing it, of seeing if you can make magic from an empty page and a pen. The truth is that it is not a trick. It is an art and a craft and a marvellous magic, and I long with every story to understand it better and to do it better too.

(2009, Paper 1, Section 1, Reading)

Questions

1. In this passage the writer mentions a number of elements that enable him to write.

   (a) Identify two of these elements.   (5 marks)

   (b) Basing your answer on the passage, explain how one of these elements contributes to the writing of his stories.   (10 marks)

2. In paragraph six Morpurgo says 'the story will be written when the moment is right'. From your reading of the passage what do you think he means by this comment?   (10 marks)

3. Do you think Morpurgo enjoys being a writer? Give reasons for your answer.
                                                           (15 marks)

2 Personal Writing

Read	Revised	Recapped

aims
- To write **clear sentences**.
- To build **coherent paragraphs**.
- To choose the correct **content**.
- To **plan** logically.
- To understand a variety of **styles**.

The Personal Writing question is the most important question on Paper 1 and carries **70 marks** out of the total 180 for the whole paper. You will spend **one hour** on this question.

The **key skills** in essay writing are:
- Construct proper **sentences** and **paragraphs**.
- **Choose the best material** for your essay. Your content must be **interesting, relevant** and **original.**
- Write a **good plan** for your composition.
- Be familiar with a **variety of styles** of personal writing.
- **Develop your plan** into a top-class composition.
- Use interesting **quotations** or **proverbs**.
- Recognise technical **figures of speech**.

Sentences

Sentences are the building blocks of all writing. When we communicate clearly, we are using words correctly to form sentences. Sentences can be **statements**, **commands** or **questions**.

Sentences must include:
1. **Subject:** The subject is **who** or **what** the sentence is about.
2. **Finite verb:** A finite verb is a **verb that has a subject**.
3. **Complete sense:** A group of words together **must make sense** in order to function as a sentence.

Rome is the capital city of Italy.
The **subject** here is 'Rome', the **finite verb** is the verb 'to be' ('is') and no additional words or phrases are needed for the sentence to **make sense**. This sentence is a **statement** and most of your writing is composed of statements.

PUNCTUATE!
Every sentence must **begin** with a **capital letter** and **end** with a **full stop**, **exclamation mark** or **question mark**.

Is Rome the capital of Italy?
The **subject** is still 'Rome' and the **verb** is still 'to be' ('is'). These six words together have a **clear meaning**. This time the sentence is a **question**. Always add a question mark to the end of a question, even a **rhetorical** question.

A **rhetorical** question is one that needs **no** answer, e.g. 'If you tickle us, do we not laugh?'

Fly to Rome immediately!
In this sentence, the **subject is implied**. The reader understands that a word such as 'you' has been left out to convey a **sense of urgency**. The verb 'to fly' is in the **imperative mood** and the four words together form a clear command.

The **imperative** is the form of a **verb** expressing an **order**, e.g. **'Do** it!', **'Come** here!', **'Get** back!'

Everything you write relies on sentences. If your sentences are correctly written, then the reader will understand them. While sentences are basic units of language, paragraphs are about **developing** ideas, **explaining**, **illustrating** or **expanding** them at length.

Paragraphs

All the sentences in a paragraph are linked by a **common idea, theme or concept.** When you have explored or developed one idea and are ready to move on to the

A **paragraph** is a **group of sentences** with a **united purpose**.

next, you must begin with a new paragraph. This is essential to give your reader a sense of the **logical organisation** of the essay. Good paragraphing helps the reader to have a clear idea of the **shape** and **purpose** of your composition.

When you plan your composition well, it helps to give you an image of the overall arrangement of your paragraphs. At the planning stage, you should also think about **how you will link or connect one paragraph to the next.**

The paragraph usually begins with a **key sentence** from which **all the other sentences flow.** Key sentences establish an idea and the **subsequent sentences** in a paragraph **develop,** expand, explain or illustrate these initial ideas. Look carefully at the following three paragraphs taken from the travel book *In Patagonia*, written by Bruce Chatwin.

> A Boer gave me a lift back south, through Perito Moreno, to Arroyo Feo, where the volcanic badlands began. He was a veterinary surgeon and he didn't think much of the other Boers.
>
> A frill of pleated white cliffs danced round the horizon. The surface of the ground was blotched with scabs of dribbling magenta. I spent the night with a road gang whose caravans sat inside a ring of yellow bulldozers. The men were eating greasy fritters and asked me to share them. Perón smirked over the company.
>
> Among them was a Scot with ginger hair and the physique of a caber thrower. He peered at me with milky-blue eyes, feeling out affinities of race and background with a mixture of curiosity and pain. His name was Robbie Ross.

- The first paragraph **identifies** the motorist who drove Chatwin to 'Arroyo Feo'. It contains only two sentences, the second of which gives more detail about the man.
- Once he changes to **describing the place**, he begins a **new paragraph**. All five sentences in the second paragraph are **linked** because they give us information about Arroyo Feo.
- He begins a third paragraph when he introduces a **new character**, Robbie Ross. Always begin a **new paragraph** when you **change character, event, time** or **location**.

Descriptive paragraphs

In the paragraph below, the writer Joe O'Connor is **describing** a disco he used to attend as a teenager.

> It used to be the last song of the night at the Presentation College disco, Glasthule, where I first strutted my funky stuff. 'Prez', as it was known, was a pretty rough joint. They searched you outside for strong drink and offensive weapons and if you didn't have any, they didn't let you in. But 'Stairway to Heaven' reduced even the most hardened knackers, savage boot boys and nefarious ne'er-do-wells to wide-eyed blubbing wrecks. I can still see it now, a great head-banging mass of denim and cheesecloth and existential angst.

- The initial sentence **identifies** the disco.
- All the other sentences in the paragraph help that first sentence by giving **more precise detail**.
- Always illustrate your points well, giving **clear** and **accurate examples**.

Autobiographical paragraphs

In an autobiographical- or memoir-style essay, your content should be drawn from your **own personal experience**. You must write in the **first person,** using 'I'. The following paragraph is taken from *Pictures in My Head*, the memoir of the Irish film star Gabriel Byrne. Here Gabriel recreates the **detail** and **sensations** of his first trip to the cinema in the company of his granny. Notice how well this paragraph illustrates this experience by reference to **images of light, colour and movement.**

Images are mental pictures created by the writer.

> All around the foyer there were painted photographs of men with black moustaches and women with bright red lipstick like my mother. Then the sentry pulled back the door and we were in darkness with the noise of those strange voices all around us. We edged our way along by a wall **like blind people**, me holding on to her coat for fear, till suddenly in an explosion of blinding colour, I saw before me the bluest sea I could ever imagine, and on it two huge boats with sails, sailing under a vast blueness of sky. I turned my head in terror into her body, and for an eternity of moments I dared not look again. When I opened my eyes, I saw a light beam in the darkness and a voice asked for our tickets, as it came toward us. And with her arm around me, we followed the dancing light as it lit our way along the steps, till we found our seats and I sat down overwhelmed by the fear and the mystery and the magic of it all. But as the wonder grew, the terror died. And so I came to know the lovely dark womb of the picture-house for the first time.

Simile: The author **compares** the way they moved to the cautious motion of the blind.

- This paragraph **paints a picture** of a key moment from the writer's childhood.
- The pronouns 'I' and 'we' tell us it is a **personal** recollection or memoir.
- The writer captures the excitement through attention to details of **sensation** and **emotion**.
- The last sentence gives us a curious **image**, the **metaphor** of the cinema as a 'womb', suggesting comfort and security.

Narrative paragraphs

Short stories are **not autobiographical** when the characters and events are **fiction** that is invented. In a short story, start a **new paragraph** every time you switch to a **new location, time, event, or character.** Every **new line** of **dialogue** should also begin a **new paragraph.** The episode on the next page is taken from a short story called 'Snot's Green Sea' by Frances Cotter. Notice that the extract is made up of **nine separate paragraphs.**

After the MP3 incident, I was more tuned into Snot. (That's nearly a joke . . . I think . . . tuned in . . . like on a radio . . . except it's an MP3 player.) I was really keen to know what was on the machine.

Once, in the dressing room, I saw his jacket and slipped my hand in his pocket. I felt the cool, rectangular shape and the two thin leads. I rummaged for the switch and was just about to turn it on, when BANG!

I was on the ground. My ear was bursting as if it was filled with hot chilli sauce. For a second I thought the earplug was a booby trap like a 007 device, but then I saw Snot's white knuckles.

'Don't you ever touch my stuff. Do you hear?'

'But Snot, I just wanted to –'

'It's none of your business!'

His face was very near mine.

'Okay Snot, I was just wondering . . . I won't –'

I was on my feet and running.

Short paragraphs are used here for the following reasons:

- The **change of location** to the dressing room requires a new paragraph.
- There is a new paragraph to show the **boy's reaction** to being hit on the head.
- **Each line of dialogue** is given a new paragraph to show that a different character is speaking.
- The final line is a new paragraph because a **new action** is happening as the boy runs away.
- Short sentences and paragraphs help to give the passage a quick and energetic **pace.**

Remember:

- Every short story should **include some dialogue.**
- **Do not include too much dialogue.** A good writer will use direct speech sparingly.
- Choose a **key moment** in the story to have characters speak aloud to each other.
- The spoken words should be **important.**

Choosing your material and planning

The skill of good writing begins with **methodical, clear thinking.** When you are given a list of composition titles, you must select wisely by deciding which task suits you best.

Write about what you know

Answer the following **three questions** on a sheet of paper before you do the exam. Your answers should be **precise.** Answering these questions honestly will help you to **identify**

the topics you should write about in your exam compositions.

- Name **three** things you **feel passionately** about.
- Name the **three topics** you **know best**.
- What are your **three clearest memories?**

The nine areas you have now identified are all **topics you know well**. In the case of the things you feel passionately about, they are aspects of your life and experience where you have formed **strong opinions** based on what you know and understand. An example of this could be: 'Dangerous Driving on the Roads of Ireland'. Your knowledge of recent accidents or intense emotions related to your own personal memories of dangerous driving have informed your view. So if you write about it, you will be drawing on these experiences to explain your position.

Brainstorming

One good way to select content for your composition during the exam is to brainstorm. This means to jot down all the random words that come to mind when you think of a topic. Use the composition title to identify all the **key words** and list the **things you associate** with that word or phrase.

Look through the ideas in the diagram above and find any possible **links**:
- The references to Lionel Messi and Croke Park are both **sports related**.
- There are two points that appeal to the **senses**: taste and smell.
- There are three specific **places** mentioned: two in Dublin and one in Europe.
- The remaining references are linked, as they evoke ideas of glamour and shopping.

Finding links between ideas helps you to plan where and when to use certain paragraphs. Each new paragraph should follow on from the previous one to **give shape** to your composition.

Giving shape to your composition

Organise the points for your essay into a logical sequence:

1. **Introduction:** Tell the reader what you aim to do.

2. **Body of the composition:**
    (a) Heavenly tastes: Magnum Double Caramel.
    (b) The scent of paradise: Eternity perfume.
    (c) Croke Park in September: Heaven on earth.
    (d) An angel come to inspire us: Lionel Messi.
    (e) Dreamland for children: Disneyland Paris.
    (f) Consumers on cloud nine: Dundrum Shopping Centre.
    (g) Paying for paradise: A platinum credit card.
    (h) My celebrity wedding: A heavenly banquet; guest list.

3. **Conclusion:** Remind the reader about what you have said.

These three sections are the essential parts of every essay. A good essay is shaped like a sandwich: the introduction and conclusion are the two slices of bread and the body of the composition is the filling!

Introduction
- Begin with a strong, confident sentence.
- Outline the range or scope of your essay.
- Let the reader know what to expect later.

Body of the composition
- Points a–h above are the body of your composition.
- All points must be relevant to the title.
- Six to eight paragraphs is a good guideline.

Conclusion
- Bring together your points in the last paragraph.
- Remind the reader of what you have already written.

Planning a short story

The key to a short story lies in the name. Its shortness obviously refers to the length. In the exam you may write **up to four pages** in the answer book in the hour available to you. The story is also limited in the sense that you can only really develop **one** central character and your plot will build up to a single dramatic moment or **climax**.

There is neither the space nor the time to develop a complex storyline or a wonderfully rich and varied cast of characters.

Setting

Create a convincing picture of a setting: the **time** and **place** of your story. Use images to help your reader enter the world of your story.

Character

Develop the main character in the story. First person 'I' narratives allow you greater freedom to explore the thoughts and feelings of this person, as well as their appearance and behaviour.

Conflict

Give the character a **problem**. This part of your story is where the main action or conflict occurs. Usually the conflict takes the form of a clash between characters. Here there ought to be a significant piece of **dialogue**: short but crucial to the climax of the story. The climax is the moment of greatest tension in your short story.

Resolution

Bring the story to a clear end by showing some **consequence** of the climax. Read 'The Ring' by Bryan MacMahon on p. 135 for a good example of this structure in practice.

Using pictures to build stories

The exam question may ask you to tell a story based on a photograph or picture. Use the picture as a launching pad for your short story.

Setting

- Think about the **information** given in the picture, e.g. time and place.
- Pay attention to the **details** of landscape, weather and buildings.
- Use the detail to create an interesting world for your short story.

Character

- Use **details** of the clothing, posture, gestures and expression of people in the photo to describe your characters.
- Remember, in your short story there is **one** key individual who is at the heart of the narrative.
- Give that person a range of private thoughts and feelings.
- Avoid any tendency to rush into describing a sequence of actions.
- Keep the plot very short and simple.

Conflict

- Are there two or more people who could be in **conflict**?
- You can **invent** a separate character outside the photo, who can come into conflict with the main character.
- Keep the action **simple**.
- Always include some **dialogue**. This helps to create a real sense of drama and contrast.

Resolution

- The last paragraph shows how the conflict **unravels**.
- Imagine the photo is the **final** scene in the story.
- A photo is a frozen image of **one moment**; the whole story may lead up to that point.

PRACTISE THE SKILL!

Write a short story based on what you see in this photograph.

SAMPLE OPENING PARAGRAPH

Even as I blew the whistle, I knew this was the biggest mistake of my life. It was a fair challenge, the Arizona player had clearly stolen the ball. Any contact she made was fair, within the rules of basketball. The Texas power-forward cried out as she fell, and in that instant my impulse was to award the free. It was in the last seconds of the National Colleges Final and the teams were level at 72 points each. A score for Texas would give them the championship for the first time ever and deny Arizona a record-breaking three in a row. I was referee in the most important match of my career and it looked like it could be my last.

COMMENT

This writer takes an interesting **perspective** on the dramatic photograph. The person telling the story is central to the game but outside the frame of this shot. The writer has chosen to start the short story from the moment the picture was taken and the **suspense** of the occasion is captured well in the opening paragraph.

Writing a speech

One common type of composition is a speech to be delivered on some momentous occasion.

> **key point**
>
> The skill is to write in a **style** suitable for your audience and for the occasion.

For example, a victory speech delivered by the captain of a county camogie team will differ greatly in tone to a formal debate for or against the motion that *Irish People Do Not Make Foreigners Feel Welcome*. The setting for the second speech is likely to be more **formal** and the language and style should reflect this.

Regardless of the purpose of your speech, the **techniques of persuasion** are the same.

The speech below illustrates this very well. It was delivered by George W. Bush shortly after the terrorist attacks on the Twin Towers of the World Trade Center in September 2001. The speech is analysed for you and various techniques are highlighted.

> **key point**
>
> Your **aims** are:
> - To express strong personal **opinions**.
> - To arouse intense **emotion** in your audience.

Address to the Nation
11 September 2001

Good evening. Today, **our** fellow citizens, **our** way of life, **our** very freedom came under attack in a series of deliberate and deadly terrorist acts. The victims were in airplanes, or in their offices; secretaries, businessmen and women, military and federal workers; moms and dads, friends and neighbours.

Thousands of lives were suddenly ended by evil, despicable acts of terror. The pictures of airplanes flying into buildings, fires burning, huge structures collapsing, have filled us with disbelief, terrible sadness, and a quiet, unyielding anger. These acts of mass murder were intended to frighten our nation into chaos and retreat. But they have failed; our country is strong.

A great people has been moved to defend a great nation. Terrorist attacks can shake the foundations of our biggest buildings, but they cannot touch the foundation of America. These acts shattered steel, but they cannot dent the steel of American resolve. America was targeted for attack because we're the brightest beacon for freedom and opportunity in the world. And no one will keep that light from shining.

Today, our nation saw evil, the very worst of human nature. And we responded with the best of America – with the daring of our rescue workers, with the caring for strangers and neighbours who came to give blood and help in any way they could.

Immediately following the first attack, I implemented our government's emergency response plans. Our military is powerful, and it's prepared. Our emergency teams are working in New York City and Washington, D.C. to help with local rescue efforts.

Our first priority is to get help to those who have been injured, and to take every precaution to protect our citizens at home and around the world from further attacks. The functions of our government continue without interruption. Federal agencies in Washington, which had to be evacuated today, are reopening for essential personnel tonight, and will be open for business tomorrow. Our financial institutions remain strong, and the American economy will be open for business, as well.

The search is underway for those who are behind these evil acts. I've directed the full resources of our intelligence and law enforcement communities to find those responsible and to bring them to justice. We will make no distinction between the terrorists who committed these acts and those who harbour them.

I appreciate so very much the members of Congress who have

Repetition of the word 'our' emphasises the point.

Emotive language and imagery ('moms and dads') manipulates the reader's feelings.

Alliteration is used for emphasis ('biggest buildings').

Imagery is used to convey hope ('brightest beacon...And no one will keep that light from shining').

Positive words put the audience at ease ('help' and 'protect').

joined me in strongly condemning these attacks. And on behalf of the American people, I thank the many world leaders who have called to offer their condolences and assistance. America and our friends and allies join with all those who want peace and security in the world, and we stand together to win the war against terrorism.

> **Buzz words** and slogans are used to make speeches more memorable ('win the war against terrorism').

Tonight, I ask for your prayers for all those who grieve, for the children whose worlds have been shattered, for all whose sense of safety and security has been threatened. And I pray they will be comforted by a power greater than any of us, spoken through the ages in Psalm 23: 'Even though I walk through the valley of the shadow of death, I fear no evil, for You are with me.'

> **Quotation** is used to evoke the power and authority of tradition.

This is a day when all Americans from every walk of life unite in our resolve for justice and peace. America has stood down enemies before, and we will do so this time. None of us will ever forget this day. Yet, we go forward to defend freedom and all that is good and just in our world.

This speech was written in response to a dramatic moment in the life of a nation. The aim of the writer was to unify the American people in the aftermath of this traumatic event. **Repetition** is used in a variety of ways. The first person pronoun 'I' is used sparingly. Instead, the writer uses 'we', 'our' and 'us', helping to create a **sense of unity** between the people and their president. Short emphatic **slogans** reassure the people that their country is strong. **Emotive** language and **buzz words** give vent to intense feelings of outrage or sympathy. It is most persuasive to appeal to the **heart**, rather than the head, in the midst of a crisis.

Tips for good speech writing

- Always keep the **audience** in mind.
- Address the audience **directly** and **frequently** in the course of the speech.
- Try to **use images** to crystallise the feeling of the moment. In the speech above, the imagery of light is used to suggest the virtue of the American way of life and to imply the darkness, ignorance and cruelty of America's enemies.
- Use good **metaphors** to draw together key ideas and feelings in your speech.
- The **style** of language used must suit the audience; a formal gathering requires a serious tone, whereas a speech to family or friends may involve colloquial language and an intimate tone.
- Give concrete **examples** to illustrate your points.
- **Conclude** your speech in a confident manner.

Write a speech to be delivered to a third year assembly, for or against the motion that *Transition Year Should Be Made Compulsory.*   (70 marks)

(2005, Paper 1, Section 2, Personal Writing)

Writing a personal discursive composition

The composition title will sometimes allow you to explore and discuss your **personal view** on a topic. The earlier exercise in **writing about what you know** will help you to identify the most interesting material available to you.

One other technique is to simply write a list of **ten short sentences**, each beginning with 'I'. For an essay title about hope, you would write ten simple sentences, each beginning with 'I hope'.

- Make the sentences **specific**.
- Include one **personal** hope.
- Include a hope relating to your **family**.
- Think of one hope focused on **your local area**.
- Use one hope for the **nation** of Ireland.
- Include one international or **global** hope.

Now arrange these ideas in a **plan**, by finding **links** between them and imposing a logical sequence or **order** on your examples. Don't worry if you decide not to use two or three; the remaining points will be enough for a good composition.

Planning answers

The composition below by Rebecca Smyth was planned using the strategy of writing ten short sentences, each beginning with the words **'I hate'**. In selecting her best ideas, she focused on **four main points** and in her essay she elaborates well on these. Notice also the way the **initial sentences** in her paragraphs establish **links** between the key examples in the essay. The introduction and conclusion are short and sharply focused on the key idea of the title 'My Pet Hates'.

My Pet Hates

Rebecca Smyth

Pop bands, arachnids, Business Studies and certain aspects of DIY. 'What do they have in common?' I hear you cry. Well, I'll tell you. I hate every last one of them passionately.

The first one may seem to be a rather sweeping generalisation, so I will clarify that point. I am not a po-faced *NME* journalist-in-waiting. By no means. I even like the Sugababes! I do, however, really hate the Pussycat Dolls. This group of smirking, scantily-clad airheads irk me no end. Their music epitomises all that is rubbish in the charts and their attitude is that of Generation X-Factor. Where once we had Generation X (the lads wore baggy clothes, the girls smelled like teen spirit and their hero was Kurt Cobain), we now have Generation X-Factor (the girls wear barely any clothes, the lads smell like Lynx and their hero is . . . Jodie Marsh!). Although Generation X were hardly the cheeriest of folk and Cobain wasn't exactly an ideal role model, I sincerely doubt that Jordan is in the running for the Spokesperson of a Generation Award. The times are indeed a-changin' when it comes to pop culture.

Far worse than the parasites feeding on the cult of celebrity are the actual creatures that feed on literal parasites. I mean, of course, spiders. They inspire both intense fear and revulsion in me. The worst thing about them is their knack of appearing in the most unexpected places at the most inconvenient times. The way they move frankly terrifies me. They arch their spindly black legs and delicately crawl along walls, ceilings, floors – everywhere. Their habit of bouncing merrily along a silky thread, threatening to drop on one's head, as they spiral and bumble up and down a web, sends me shrieking across county borders in a bid to escape them. Nature programmes concerning spiders have the same effect on me. The close-ups of their compound eyes, each crackling click of their movements exaggerated, the horrible facts (for example, 'the Goliath bird-eating spider can grow up to the size of a dinner plate') truly disgust me. Don't try to convince me that spiders do a necessary job, or that money spiders are lucky or that small spiders are 'cute'. I've heard it all before and nothing will persuade me that spiders are not super-scary, repulsive creatures who would cheerfully eat me alive!

More odious than poisonous tarantulas is the most loathsome of all subjects on the school curriculum: Business Studies! Those two words send a chill of boredom down my spine, tedium so intense that it makes the riff of Coldplay's 'Talk' seem almost electrifying. Not only are final accounts, double-entry bookkeeping and bank statements needlessly complicated, when one of the above doesn't balance, poor put-upon students feel like weeping, tearing their hair out, sending death threats to the author of Business Studies textbooks everywhere or going out to find out what's on the telly. To make matters worse, the course is never-ending and features such treasure troves of information and enjoyment as: 'calculating insurance premiums', 'how to form a private limited company' and much more besides! The cherry on the cake is that business is so worthwhile and important – I feel guilty for hating it because it's so necessary to, well, everything. What kind of fine upstanding young lady ready to take her place in the world am I if I don't learn about economic systems? That's right – a happy one!

As you may have guessed, one of the career options I have ruled out is an entrepreneur. Another is anything involving drilling. The incessant whinge of a drill, as it intensifies from low whine to high keen, drives me insane (or up the wall if you'll excuse the building-related pun!). The behaviour that drilling entails is also a tad disturbing. Perfectly sane, reasonable, soft-spoken men turn into professionals on spark plugs, plasterboard, faulty elbow joints in piping and other such fascinating 'structural flaws' as soon as they pick up a drill. The journey to Woodie's DIY on a Sunday and the inexplicable desire to buy discount chipboard are other side effects of excessive DIY-ing. The appeal of 'home improvement' (the euphemism for DIY) is that the drill handler is now alpha male, taking on all blocked drains, cracked ceilings and suchlike. The flaw in DIY is that the drill bearer is usually a walking liability. Male pride takes over and cries of 'It's supposed to look like that!' abound when one is fool enough to question the large hole in the wall or submersion of the kitchen floor due to a drilled-through pipe. The helpful suggestion ('Maybe you should call a builder?') will not be well received. It is taken as a direct challenge to the driller's masculinity. Yes indeed, DIY is truly a mixed blessing.

The only solution to my pet hates are:

(a) I go to live in a remote, spider-free cave, removed from society, devoid of all mechanical drilling devices and copies of *Business Studies for Beginners*.

(b) I get myself deported so that only penguins will have to listen to me complaining.

(c) I take anger management courses. Or perhaps I could express all my feelings in an essay entitled 'My Pet Hates'.

Use the same strategy to plan and write a composition entitled 'Heroes'.
To plan it, write ten sentences beginning with 'I admire'.

Quotations

Sometimes it helps to **begin** an essay with a curious, provocative or humorous quotation. The following is a list of quotations, arranged according to themes. Read them and **learn** any you particularly like. You may find them useful later in composing your introduction to an essay. When choosing a quotation, learn to ask yourself whether you have opinions of your own that will help to develop a paragraph beginning with this line. Over time **build up your own store of quotations** – a very helpful resource for the student of English.

Sport

'Games are for people who can neither read nor think.' *G.B. Shaw*

'Some people think football is a matter of life and death. I assure them it is much more serious that that!' *Bill Shankly*

'When you win, nothing hurts.' *Joe Namath*

'Swifter, higher, stronger.' *Olympic motto*

'Golf is a day spent in a round of strenuous idleness.' *William Wordsworth*

'Football is all very well as a game for rough girls, but it is hardly suitable for sensitive boys.' *Oscar Wilde*

'He had ice in his veins, warmth in his heart, and timing and balance in his feet.' *Danny Blanchflower, of George Best*

'Playing a cheater is a real test of sportsmanship.' *Jack Barnaby*

Religion and science

'. . . one small step for [a] man, one giant leap for mankind.' *Neil Armstrong*

'Art and religion are means to similar states of mind.' *Clive Bell*

'Art is meant to disturb, science reassures.' *Georges Braque*

'Science without religion is lame, religion without science is blind.' *Albert Einstein*

'Science is nothing but trained and organised common sense.' *Thomas Henry Huxley*

Books

'A good book has no ending.' *R.D. Cumming*

'Books think for me.' *Charles Lamb*

'If a book is worth reading, it is worth buying.' *John Ruskin*

'Reading is sometimes an ingenious device for avoiding thought.' *Arthur Helps*

'I am a part of all that I have read.' *John Kieran*

'A book is a garden carried in the pocket.' *Chinese proverb*

'The proper study of mankind is books.' *Aldous Huxley*

'A book should teach us to enjoy life, or to endure it.' *Samuel Johnson*

Stages of life

'Every man desires to live long; but no man would be old.' *Jonathan Swift*

'Old age is the most unexpected of all things that happen to a man.' *Leon Trotsky*

'The aim of education is the knowledge not of facts but of values.' *William R. Inge*

'Youth would be an ideal state if it came a little later in life.' *H.H. Asquith*

Human qualities

'No one can make you feel inferior without your consent.' *Eleanor Roosevelt*

'He who never hoped can never despair.' *G.B. Shaw*

'Man is the only animal that blushes. Or needs to.' *Mark Twain*

'All sins are attempts to fill voids.' *Simone Weil*

'We are all born mad. Some remain so.' *Samuel Beckett*

'In dreams begin responsibilities.' *W.B. Yeats*

'Humankind cannot bear very much reality.' *T.S. Eliot*

'Love is like the measles; we all have to go through it.' *Jerome K. Jerome*

'We must love one another or die.' *W.H. Auden*

'I have always depended on the kindness of strangers.' *Blanche DuBois,* A Streetcar Named Desire

Political affairs

'All human beings are born free and equal in dignity and rights.' *United Nations*

'Money doesn't talk, it swears.' *Bob Dylan*

'Mankind must put an end to war or war will put an end to mankind.' *John F. Kennedy*

'Injustice anywhere is a threat to justice everywhere.' *Martin Luther King*

'In violence we forget who we are.' *Mary McCarthy*

'When war is declared, truth is the first casualty.' *Arthur Ponsonby*

'There is no such thing as society.' *Margaret Thatcher*

'Politics come from man. Mercy, compassion and justice come from God.' *Terry Waite*

'Knowledge itself is power.' *Francis Bacon*

The Arts and Media

'The secret of art is in life.' *Oscar Wilde*

'If music be the food of love, play on!' *William Shakespeare*

'A great artist can paint a great picture on a small canvas.' *Charles Dudley Warner*

'Where the press is free and every man is able to read, all is safe.' *Thomas Jefferson*

'The medium is the message.' *Marshall McLuhan*

'A good newspaper is a nation talking to itself.' *Arthur Miller*

'You can tell the ideals of a nation by its advertisements.' *Norman Douglas*

'Poetry is a way of taking life by the throat.' *Robert Frost*

'A thing of beauty is a joy forever.' *John Keats*

'A poet is the painter of the soul.' *Isaac D'Israeli*

Proverbs

Proverbs are pithy expressions of **traditional wisdom**. You can also quote them in your compositions and you may choose to challenge or contradict the opinions they articulate.

Many hands make light work.

If at first you don't succeed, try and try again.

A watched pot never boils.

Absence makes the heart grow fonder.

Love makes the world go round.

When in Rome do as the Romans do.

A bird in the hand is worth two in the bush.

A friend in need is a friend indeed.

All work and no play makes Jack a dull boy.

An apple a day keeps the doctor away.

Never judge a book by its cover.

Half a loaf is better than none.

It's the little things in life that count.

Variety is the spice of life.

Figures of speech

The following terms or figures of speech are used when interpreting or analysing poems, plays or stories. You may not need to use all of these terms, but the list covers a wide range of technical words and offers a short explanation of what each one means.

Allegory: A story or poem with two levels of meaning, one literal level and a second parallel or hidden meaning.

Alliteration: Repetition of consonants, especially at the beginning of words close to one another.

Allusion: A reference in a poem or story to some character or event in another poem or story.

Ambiguity: When a word, phrase or sentence is open to more than one meaning or interpretation.

Anticlimax: When the climax or crisis in a story disappoints or fails to deliver an exciting result.

Assonance: The repetition of identical vowel sounds in words that appear close to one another.

Ballad: A poem telling a dramatic story in simple language, involving dialogue and action, often with a chorus or refrain and usually with a tragic outcome.

Cacophony: Repetition of harsh sounds in a poem or story.

Catastrophe: The tragic outcome in a drama.

Character: A person in a poem, story or drama.

Colloquial: Informal language close to the vocabulary and style of everyday speech.

Comedy: A play or story written to amuse the audience by highlighting the foolishness of people. The ending is usually a happy one.

Conflict: The tension in a situation between characters in a story, poem or drama.

Couplet: A pair of rhyming lines, usually of equal length, in a poem or play.

Crossed rhyme: When a word in the middle of a line of poetry rhymes with a word in the middle of the next line.

Dialogue: Words spoken by characters in a poem, story or drama.

Diction: The choice of words or vocabulary in a story, poem or drama.

Elegy: A mournful poem or lament.

Emotive: Language used to arouse intense feeling in the reader or audience.

Enjambment: A run-on line in poetry, where the sense of one line runs into the next.

Epic: A long narrative tale of adventure usually involving a journey undertaken by a courageous and resourceful hero.

Eponymous: When the name or the hero or heroine is also the title of the story, e.g. *Romeo and Juliet*.

Euphony: The repetition of pleasant or sweet sounds in a poem, story or play.

Fable: A very short story, often involving animal characters whose actions and attitudes resemble human characteristics. They usually have a moral lesson.

Fiction: Invented stories, poems or plays.

Genre: The type or category a story fits into, e.g. thriller, comedy or horror.

Hero/heroine: The central character in a story, poem or play, usually a noble person who saves the day.

Hyperbole: Gross exaggeration for the sake of emphasis.

Imagery: The images or mental pictures created by a writer in a poem, story or play.

Interior monologue: When the thoughts of a character in a story, poem or play are written down directly without any break or interruption.

Irony: When there is a contrast between literal meaning and actual meaning.

Lament: A poem expressing deep regret over the loss or death of something loved.

Legend: A story passed down from ancient times involving superhuman heroic deeds and mythical creatures.

Logo: A symbol representing a particular brand or company, often used in advertising.

Lyric: A short poem expressing the feelings and thoughts of a single speaker.

Metaphor: When one thing is described in terms of another; a comparison.

Metre: The pattern of stressed and unstressed syllables in poetry.

Monologue: A speech by one person only.

Mood: The feeling or state of mind created by a poem or story.

Narrative: A story.

Narrator: The storyteller.

Octave: The first eight lines in a Petrarchan sonnet.

Onomatopoeia: When the sound of a word echoes its meaning, e.g. fizz, plop, moo.

Paradox: A contradiction in a poem or story.

Parallelism: The repetition of words in a sentence to give balance or symmetry, often used in slogans.

Parody: A mocking imitation of a certain style of poem, story or play.

Pastoral: Poems, stories and plays set in idyllic rural settings, often featuring characters from country life, e.g. shepherds.

Pathetic fallacy: When something inanimate is imagined to have human feelings.

Personification: When an object, animal or idea is described as if it were a person.

Plot: The pattern of events in a story.

Point of view: In cinema and TV this means a shot taken from the viewpoint of a particular character.

Prose: Text that is not written in verse form.

Quatrain: A group or stanza of four rhymed or unrhymed lines. Shakespearean sonnets have three quatrains and a rhyming couplet.

Register: The style of language suitable in a particular social situation – formal for a formal audience, informal for a more intimate audience.

Rhetorical question: A question that does not require an answer, used for the sake of persuasive effect.

Rhyme: In poetry, when two or more words, usually at the end of the line, have the same or similar sounds.

Rhythm: The pattern of sound in a line of poetry, the 'beat' of the line.

Satire: A style of writing that aims to make a person or group of people appear ridiculous.

Scene: In a play, the subdivision of an act; all the action in a particular place at a particular time.

Sestet: The last six lines of a Petrarchan sonnet.

Setting: The fictional time and place where a story is set.

Simile: A comparison using the words 'like' or 'as'.

Soliloquy: A speech in a drama where the character delivers his or her own thoughts and feelings directly to the audience.

Sonnet: A poem of fourteen lines. Petrarchan sonnets divide the lines into two groups: the octave and the sestet. Shakespearean sonnets divide the lines into four quatrains and a rhyming couplet at the end.

Stanza: A separate group of lines in a poem; a verse.

Stereotype: An exaggerated or unjustified representation of a group of people, e.g. racial stereotypes are unfair depictions of people of the same nationality.

Subplot: A secondary sequence of events in a story or play, usually involving minor characters.

Symbol: An object in a poem, play or story which stands for something else.

Synonym: A word similar in meaning to another word.

Syntax: The order in which words are arranged in a sentence.

Theme: A key idea explored in a poem, story or play.

Tone: The reflection of the writer's attitude in a poem, play or story.

Tragedy: A drama dealing with a serious issue, involving a crisis for the hero or heroine and resulting in an unhappy ending, often with the deaths of several characters.

Verse: Poetry; or a particular group of lines in a poem.

Villain: The principal evil character in a story.

Write a prose composition on any **one** of the following titles. Except where otherwise stated, you are free to write in any form you wish, e.g. narrative, descriptive, dramatic, short story, etc.

(70 marks)

1. Magical moments from my childhood.

2. My secret life as a superhero.

3. Things that make me angry.

4. Write a composition including the line: 'That really was the last straw.'

5. Write a speech for **OR** against the motion: *Mobile Phones Should Be Banned in Schools*.

6. The rudest person I have ever met.

7. Look at the photo that accompanies this question and write a composition inspired by it.

REMEMBER YOUR AIMS!
- Clear sentences.
- Coherent paragraphs.
- Choosing correct content.
- Logical planning.
- Variety of style.

(2009, Paper 1, Section 2, Personal Writing)

Read	Revised	Recapped

- To learn the **structure** of various forms of functional writing.
- To **analyse** samples of functional writing.
- To **practise** answering functional writing questions.

The Functional Writing section of Paper 1 deals with a wide variety of writing **styles**. You will be given a choice of at least **two** different types of writing tasks. It is vital to **practise several** different types of functional writing. This unit will give you guidelines on writing:

- Diaries.
- Letters.
- Reviews.
- Reports.
- Instructions.

Good functional writing begins with a clear understanding of the **purpose** of your writing. A shopping list is written for the purpose of reminding yourself what you need to buy in the shops. It should include all the items you need to purchase. It should also be brief – a lengthy description of the washing powder is unnecessary! Your list can also follow a logical order, for instance the sequence of aisles in a supermarket.

When you are sure you know the purpose of the piece of writing, ask yourself **who** the audience is. A shopping list will generally be used by the same person who wrote it. A letter, however, may be personal, intended for an intimate friend, or formally addressed to a business associate, customer or client. Letters to the editor of a newspaper are potentially read by thousands of individuals and this will influence the **style** of language and the **content** of the letter.

The audience will determine the **register** or style of a piece of functional writing. If you write a letter to your granny about your holiday in Tenerife, it should be suitably pitched for your granny.

The marks you get for functional writing are determined by how well you understand the **type of writing** you have attempted and how that understanding is reflected in the **quality of language** and **content** of your answer. For example, diaries are the most intimate and personal style of functional writing. This is because the audience is usually the person writing the diary and this gives it a more individual and confidential quality.

Remember, the marks you will earn in this section are awarded for the quality of your writing. A good answer in this section will feature:

- Suitable **layout**.
- **Logical** presentation of content.
- Good **structure**.
- **Tone** and **style** that are suitable for audience and purpose.
- Correct **grammar, spelling and punctuation**.

Purpose = what you are asked to write.
Audience = who you are writing to.
Register = how you express your ideas.

Diary entries

The key point about all diaries is that the writer is first of all recording his or her thoughts and feelings for their own private pleasure. This gives the diary a direct, intimate power, as if we are listening to the **person's own thoughts**. It also means that the writer may not need to elaborate or give

DIARIES MUST:

- Be written in the **first person**.
- Deal with **specific events**.
- Include **dates**.
- Be **chronological**.

great detail, because the diary is typically intended to act as a form of shorthand reminder of events as they happened.

Often, however, diarists are conscious that, at a later date, others will read their diary. Famous people will publish their memoirs to give the public an inside view of what the life of a celebrity involves. The diary genre creates a sense of immediacy and can provide a behind-the-scenes glimpse of important moments in the diarist's career.

On the other hand, a fictional diary uses the device of diary entries to give a sense of the **passing of time** in a character's life. A chronological development of the narrative in the first person means that we have direct access to the character's reaction to key events as they happen. We witness the gradual build-up to a climax, or even the shock of an unexpected crisis, through the hero's own personal journal.

Anyone can keep a diary, but sometimes the diary has added interest because the author is well known.

You could be asked to write a diary in the Functional Writing section, the Personal Writing section or even in response to a piece of fiction or drama in Paper 2. When composing a diary entry for a Junior Certificate question, you should give some thought to the character of the person and **why** they are keeping this diary.

- Is it to capture the detail of a **key event** in that person's life?
- Is the writer an ordinary **witness** to some momentous occasion?

- Is the character a fictional person telling his or her own **version of a short story or narrative**?
- Is this imitating a real diary based on **recent experiences in your own life**?

Once you are clear about the **purpose** of the diary, then you should write a short **plan**, identifying the number of entries and a coherent sequence of events. The register or **tone** should be **informal** and **personal**. Remember, the **first audience** for a diary is always the **writer**. It must read like an immediate, **private reaction** to real events.

A **Read the following diary of fictional character Becky Morley and answer the questions that follow.**
The third exercise requires you to write a new diary entry for a different character. Use Becky's diary as a model for the style of your answer.

The following diary entries are taken from a book called Out of the Ashes *by Michael Morpurgo. It is the diary of Becky Morley, a thirteen-year-old girl living on her parents' farm in Devon, England.*

Out of the Ashes

Michael Morpurgo

> Each entry is dated.

Saturday 24 February 2001

I decided I'd waited long enough for Ruby's foot to heal, and that it was time to try her out again, gently. I had just about enough time to groom her, saddle her up, go for a short ride and get back before dark. Bobs came along with us and we went down to the river and crossed over. The river was still high after all the rain but we managed. She went like a train up through Mr Bailey's woods and it was all I could do to rein her in at the top. She was puffing and blowing a bit, but I could tell there was nothing wrong with her foot. I was in amongst Mr Bailey's sheep and lambs before I knew it. They panicked and scattered everywhere. I just hoped Mr Bailey hadn't seen us.

By the time I'd got home, rubbed her down and fed her, it was dark. I kicked off my boots and called out that I was back. But no one said anything, and I thought that was strange because I knew they were in – I'd seen them through the window as I came past. When I went into the sitting room Mum and Dad were both sitting there just staring at a blank television screen. Neither of them even turned to look at me. I knew they were upset about something. Then I thought that Mr Bailey must have rung up to complain about me scattering his sheep, that they were furious with me. But they said nothing, just sat there. I asked what the matter was. Dad said it very quietly: 'Foot-and-mouth disease. Some pig farmer up north has got foot-and-mouth on his farm. It was on the news. They've had to kill thousands of pigs.'

> A diary is always written in the **first person**.

Thursday 1 March

Some good news. Some bad news. The good news first. At school today Mrs Merton talked about foot-and-mouth disease. She said what Mum said, that foot-and-mouth isn't likely to find its way down here to us in Devon. Last time there was an outbreak, all the cases were clustered together in Shropshire. I told Dad when I came home, but I don't think he was even listening. And there's other farmers worried like he is. On the school bus, I've seen quite a few farms with disinfected straw mats across their farm gates, and there's more and more 'Keep Out' signs. Everywhere you go now the air stinks of disinfectant. Ruby really hates it. She wrinkles up her nose whenever she smells it.

> Diary entries follow a **chronological order**.

Now the bad news. I had a bust up with Jay. I was just telling her how worried Dad was about the farm, and then she says that farmers are always moaning about something. And for no reason she goes on and on about how I had this and I had that and how I had a horse, and how I was spoilt – in front of everyone. And she's supposed to be my best friend. So I said *she* was spoilt because she's got the latest Imac computer – she's always showing it off to me when I go over to her place. Then she says if I feel like that she won't ever invite me over again. Well, who cares? God, she can be a right cow sometimes.

Monday 5 March

Up until teatime it was a great day. At school Jay came and made it up. She said she'd been a real cow, and I said I liked cows. So we're best of friends again. Then I was sitting in the kitchen having tea when Mum came in from work. She was white in the face and I soon knew why. They've discovered foot-and-mouth on a farm less than two miles away – on Speke Farm, Terry Bolan's place. She heard it on the radio in the car.

Thursday 8 March

My nightmare began this morning. I went out for a ride, just to give Ruby some exercise. We rode down through the Bluebell Wood to the river. The river bank was high again. Ruby was drinking and I was looking across the river at Mr Bailey's farm. It was deserted, not an animal in sight, just crows cawing over the wood, cackling at me as if they knew something I didn't. Suddenly, I knew what it was. The last time I'd ridden Ruby down to the river was before we knew about the foot-and-mouth. I'd crossed over on to Mr Bailey's farm. I'd galloped up through his wood and out over his sheep field. I'd been in amongst his sheep, sheep that must already have been infected with foot-and-mouth disease. I'd come home again bringing the foot-and mouth with me on Ruby, on my clothes, in my hair. We'd come back through the river, but river water isn't disinfectant. We'd carried the germs with us back to our farm. And I'd gone out with Dad checking the animals. I touched them. I helped him with the milking that evening. I milked Primrose myself. I fed Little Josh.

This is the worst feeling I've had in all my life. Ever since I first thought of what I might have done I've felt cold all over. I've been sick. All I know is that if it happens now, if we get foot-and-mouth, then it'll be all my fault.

> Each entry deals with **specific events**.

Questions

1. Imagine you are Becky's friend Jay. Now write **two diary entries** for Thursday 1 March and Monday 5 March. (30 marks)

2. Write **four** entries in the diary of an **astronaut**. Your answer should be about **200 words** in length. (30 marks)

Letter writing

The style of a letter depends on the audience or person to whom the letter is being sent. There are **three** distinct types of letter that you should practise for the exam.

- **Personal** letters.
- **Formal** letters.
- **Letters to the editor** of a newspaper.

Personal letters

Personal letters to close family members, lovers and friends will always be written in a **casual** and **intimate style**.

- The language is **informal**.
- The **content** reflects the close nature of the relationship.
- **Your address** appears on the **top right-hand** corner of the page and is followed by the **date**.
- The **greeting** should be appropriately casual or friendly and is followed by a comma.
- Begin the **body** of the letter on the next line directly beneath the greeting.
- Each new idea or subject needs a **new paragraph**.
- Your **closing salutation** will be affectionate and casual.

The following template illustrates the layout of a **personal** letter.

Your address _____ _____ _____
Today's date
Familiar greeting,
Body of the letter: one idea per paragraph
Body of the letter: one idea per paragraph
Body of the letter: one idea per paragraph
Intimate closing phrase,
Your signature

Dundalk,
Friday night

My dearest love,
I have just sent to press the last paper I will edit as a bachelor. That is a solemn thought perhaps, but I don't feel solemn about it. Four days more sweetheart!

I was over today looking for a suitable scarf and Betsy made me take a pair of gloves as well. She said I couldn't be married without gloves. I can carry them in my hands like Presbyterian shop boys going to church.

Paddy and Mrs Deery sent me a very nice present today. It is a lovely little writing table. I think it is called a Davenport. If you are very good I'll give you leave to write some letters on it.

Charlie tells me he has written Lizzie Jones in such fashion that she may honour us by turning up after all. On Charlie's account I would be glad if she did. He has a lot to learn yet, and he takes her absence as a disappointment. Not that you or I will care much! But Charlie is a good chap, and I'd like everyone to be happy on this occasion.

I am dead certain we'll forget something. I must write out a list tomorrow and check the things off. Half a dozen times I have thought of 'gold and silver' that I have to give you. I'm almost sure that will be what I'll forget at the last minute. Don't forget to enquire about hotels from Mrs O'Reilly. Frank McPartland has been telling me about a cottage that he and Martha stayed at in Glengarriff. If we're lucky we may light on such a building in Wicklow.

Good night, sweetheart. Four more days will see me the happiest man in Ireland and you I hope the happiest woman.

With love, I am, darling, your own

Tom
XXX

Question
Imagine you are Tom's fiancée. Write a **personal letter** in reply. (30 marks)

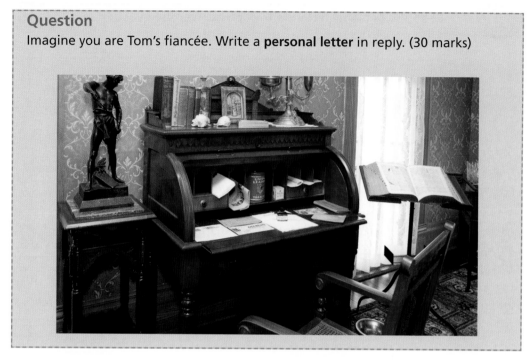

Formal letters

A formal letter is **less intimate** than a personal letter. The purpose may be to make a formal **request**, to **complain** about a faulty product or service, to **apply** for a job, or to **respond** to an important event. Your audience is a person or group with whom you have a **formal** relationship.

- The language is **formal**.
- The **content** is a matter of some importance.
- **Your address** and the **date** appear on the **top right-hand** corner.
- The **recipient's** name and address start on the following line, aligned with the **left-hand margin**.
- If you use the **recipient's name** in the greeting, the **closing salutation** should be 'Yours sincerely', followed by your **signature**.
- When you **do not use the recipient's name**, the letter concludes 'Yours faithfully', followed by your **signature**.
- 'Y' of 'Yours' is always a **capital** letter; 's' in sincerely and 'f' in faithfully are always **lower-case** letters.

The following template illustrates the layout of a **formal** letter.

Your address

_____

_____

_____

Today's date

Recipient's address

_____

_____

Formal greeting,

Body of the letter: one idea per paragraph

Body of the letter: one idea per paragraph

Body of the letter: one idea per paragraph

Formal closing phrase,

Your signature

 C Read the following letter, taken from *Adrian Mole and the Weapons of Mass Destruction* by Sue Townsend, and answer the question that follows.

Wisteria Walk
Ashby de la Zouch
Leicestershire

October 6th, 2002

Jordan
C/o *Daily Star*
Express Newspaper Group
10 Lower Thames Street
London EC3

Dear Jordan,

I am writing a book about celebrity and how it ruins people's lives. I know what I am talking about. I was a celebrity in the 1990s and had my own show on cable TV called *Offally Good!* Then the fame machine spat me out, as it will spit you out one day.

I would like to arrange an interview on a mutually convenient date. You would have to come here to Leicester because I work full-time. Sunday afternoons are good for me.

By the way, I was talking with my father about your breasts recently. We both agreed that they are very intimidating. My father said a man could fall into that cleavage and not be found for days.

My friend Parvez described them as being like Weapons of Mass Destruction, and my chiropractor predicted that you would suffer from lower back problems in the future due to the weight you were carrying on your ribcage.

It is rumoured that you are contemplating having even bigger implants inserted. I beg you to reconsider. Please contact me at the above address. I'm afraid I cannot offer a fee or expenses, but you will of course receive a free copy of the book (working title: *Celebrity and Madness*).

I remain, Madam,
Your most humble and obedient servant,

A. Mole

Question

Write a **letter to a celebrity** making a **formal request.**   (30 marks)

Letter to the editor of a newspaper or magazine

Letter pages afford readers the opportunity to **express their opinions** on topical news stories or on letters that have previously been published by the newspaper. They are different from personal and formal letters, as they are intended for a much **larger audience**.

The **style** of a letter to the editor will depend on the type of paper or magazine, but for the most part they tend to be quite serious. If you are asked to write a letter to the editor of a newspaper, the following guidelines apply.

- The letter begins with a **simple greeting** on the **left** of the page: **'Sir'** if the editor is a man, **'Madam'** if she is a woman.
- Your **name and address** appears at the **end of the closing salutation,** which is simply **'Yours, etc.'**

The following template illustrates the layout of a **letter to the editor** of a newspaper or magazine.

Today's date

Brief greeting,

Body of the letter: one idea per paragraph

Body of the letter: one idea per paragraph

Body of the letter: one idea per paragraph

Brief closing phrase,

Your signature

Your address

A national newspaper has organised a 'Person of the Year' award. Write a letter to the editor, nominating the person you think is most deserving of this award. You should explain why you think this person deserves the award.   (30 marks)

(2006, Paper 1, Section 3, Functional Writing)

SAMPLE ANSWER

31 The Rise
Ballybeg
Co. Donegal

7 June 2006

The Editor
The Irish Times
O'Connell St
Dublin 4

Dear Madam,

I am writing to you to nominate Bob Geldof for the 'Person of the Year' award that your newspaper will be organising.

I nominate Bob Geldof for the award because of his outstanding charity work. Bob Geldof single-handedly organised the Live 8 concerts around the world and spearheaded the campaign to end third world debt. Without his efforts in raising the awareness of third world debt, the results of the G8 summit might not have been as good as they were. I believe that we should show him are thanks for achieving such a goal by presenting him with this 'Person of the Year' award.

I hope you agree with my nomination of Bob Geldof and give him this award, showing him are support of what he is doing.

Yours faithfully,

Sean Bloggs

exam focus

High marks are given for:
- **Original** material.
- Correct **layout.**
- **Clear** writing.

COMMENT

This is a well-written letter. The formal layout is correctly applied, although the actual spacing of the elements of the letter is unduly compressed. The candidate nominates his subject and presents reasons in support. Some errors (e.g. 'are' for 'our') detract slightly from an otherwise accomplished piece of writing.

Now write your own answer to the letter question on p. 47, using the sample answer as a model for your own writing.

Reviews

A review is one person's **opinion** of the **quality** of a film, book, play, record or performance. It will usually appear in the pages of a magazine or newspaper and it offers the reader both **information** and a **personal response** to the work being discussed.

- **Key facts** are given in the **initial paragraphs**. In the case of a film review, this includes the **title** of the film, **names** of the **director** and key **actors** and the **genre**.
- **Central themes** are briefly outlined. Some details of **plot** are given. Not everything is **revealed** in a review, e.g. the conclusion of a mystery novel.
- **Highlights** or **key scenes** are discussed, especially if they relate to the quality of the performance of an actor or writer.
- For live performances, **lighting, sound, costume, special effects, music** and **editing** can be discussed.
- A good reviewer clearly expresses strong **personal views** on the work being reviewed.
- The reader ultimately needs to know whether you **recommend** the work or advise against seeing it.

Film reviews

 D Read this film review from *The Irish Times* and answer the question that follows.

The Irish Times: 9 January 2009
Slumdog Millionaire

This Mumbai-set rags-to-riches story is a vibrant and affecting film, writes Michael Dwyer

The most successful international television franchise in our globalised world, *Who Wants to Be a Millionaire?*, has been adapted in more than 100 countries since its UK debut in 1998. It's broadcast in any number of different languages and asks questions tailored for individual countries, but the format is the same everywhere, building tension through the multiple options for answers, the lifelines offered to contestants, and crucially, in its distinctive use of lighting and heart-thumping music.

Three years ago, French writer–director Patrice Leconte seized on the show's dramatic potential within the context of a movie when he featured it effectively towards the end of *My Best Friend*.

Now Danny Boyle goes the distance with the exhilarating *Slumdog Millionaire*, which opens in Mumbai in 2006. Teenager Jamal Malik is one question away from winning the jackpot of 20 million rupees (currently about €297,000) on the Indian version of the show. Suspicions are raised by the show's patronising presenter (Anil Kapoor) because of the uneducated young Jamal's impoverished background. As the investigation proceeds, Jamal explains how he learned each of the answers through his youthful experiences, living on the streets with his canny older brother. This is a cue for a series of seamlessly integrated flashbacks ranging from the boys witnessing their mother's murder during a violent attack on Muslims, to being groomed as beggars by adults so unscrupulous that they will gouge out a child's eyes to increase his or her earning potential.

Slumdog Millionaire is based on the novel *Q&A* by Indian author Vikas Swarup, and the film's central structural device seems contrived at first. It's almost queasily reminiscent of Wink Martindale's folksy old spoken hit single 'Deck of Cards', in which a soldier, charged with being disrespectful in church, outlines how each playing card symbolises his religious beliefs.

In the artfully-plotted screenplay by Simon Beaufoy, formerly best known for writing *The Full Monty*, Jamal's explanations prove 'bizarrely plausible', as one character describes them, and the movie exerts such a compelling hold that it defies cynicism. The brothers are played at different ages by three sets of young actors, among whom Dev Patel makes an auspicious film debut, investing the 18-year-old Jamal with a wonderfully natural exuberance. And there is an endearing chemistry between Patel and Freida Pinto as Jamal's childhood sweetheart in the movie's irresistible story of first love.

Anthony Dod Mantle's fluid, mobile camerawork captures the vitality of the teeming authentic locations as observed from Boyle's perspective as an inquisitive outsider. Boyle eschews sentimentality in unflinchingly addressing the rampant poverty of India through a Dickensian tale in which Jamal is a contemporary Oliver Twist.

This hard-edged but vibrant and affecting drama is assembled with social concern, emotional depth, dramatic urgency and an infectious energy by Boyle, the director of *Trainspotting* and *28 Days Later*, and is propelled by an exuberant music soundtrack all the way to a rousing, unforgettable finale.

Unheralded before its premiere at the Toronto festival last September, *Slumdog Millionaire* richly deserves to emulate Jamal's achievement on the TV show by taking the Oscar for Best Picture next month. If you doubt that claim, phone a friend who has seen it, or ask the audience.

* * * * *

Directed by Danny Boyle. Starring Dev Patel, Anil Kapoor, Irrfan Khan, Madhur Mittal, Freida Pinto. 15A cert, gen release, 120 min.

Question

Using Michael Dwyer's article as a model, write a review of your **favourite film**. You might like to research the film on the Internet. A useful source of facts about movies is the Internet Movie Database at www.imdb.com.

Write for your **school magazine** a review of any **one** of the following:
- A **film or video** you have seen recently.
- A favourite **tape** or **CD**.
- A **play or show** you attended.

Give the **name** of the film, video, tape, CD, play or show that you are reviewing. (30 marks)

(1995, Paper 1, Section 3, Functional Writing)

Book reviews

Book reviews are similar in **style** to film reviews.

E   **Read this book review and answer the question that follows.**

At last, a rival for J.K. and Harry
Mary Shine Thompson

Endymion Spring
By Matthew Skelton
Puffin, £12.99

Mark the names Endymion Spring and Matthew Skelton. Soon they could be as well known as Harry Potter and J.K. Rowling. Skelton's book may even give Dan Brown's *Da Vinci Code* a run for its money. Already the publishing industry has worked itself into a paroxysm about this book. No less than five publishers bid for the manuscript, and deals in six figures have been cut. The result is that Matthew Skelton, the stereotypical penniless Oxford student (he completed a doctorate on H.G. Wells), has become Skelton the successful author, with a marketable product. His book inserts itself into a tradition of children's books emanating from Oxford. It was there that C.S. Lewis conceived Narnia, and from there that Lewis Carroll's Alice (of Wonderland fame) sprang. And Oxford has drawn Phillip Pullman (remember *Lyra's Oxford*?) to it too. So how good is *Endymion Spring*? After a rather slow start, the book does live up to the publisher's hype. It is unputdownable. Never again will a library appear to be the fusty, dusty backwater of real life.

A boy called Blake is visiting Oxford with his academic mother and his kid sister called Duck. While their mum immerses herself in olde worlde volumes, Blake feels trapped in the dusty air of the college library. Until one day Blake is running his finger along the shelf and feels something pierce his finger, drawing blood – like a bite. The book responsible is a battered old volume, with a strange clasp like a serpent's head – with real fangs. Printed on its front are two words: Endymion Spring. Its dragonskin parchment paper is almost luminous – blank, wordless, but with a texture that seems to shine. The paper quivers, as if it's alive. And as Blake looks, words begin to appear on the page – words no one else can see. The book has been waiting 500 years for the right boy; now it must fulfil its destiny . . .

Interwoven with Blake's story is a story centuries earlier in the 1450s of Endymion Spring, a boy who is an apprentice to the printer Gutenburg and who saves a valuable dragonskin book from the evil Fust (the evil in the story gives it a Faustian overtone). Centuries later, when Blake comes into possession of the book, the same dark forces will stop at nothing to get their hands on it.

It comes as no surprise to learn that the film rights for *Endymion Spring* have been sold. The image of the letters of Endymion's book curling up in terror, or the battle with evil conducted on a rooftop among the gargoyles and spires, are gloriously cinematic!

Questions

Write a **review** (200 words) of **any book you have read recently,** fiction or non-fiction. Your answer could include some of the following:

- The **style** of the book.
- **Ideas** or **feelings** you had as a result of reading it.
- The **audience** most suited to reading the book.
- Your **recommendation** and the **reasons** behind it. (30 marks)

GOOD REVIEWS INCLUDE:
- Interesting **details**.
- Strong **opinions**.

Report writing

A report is a document that **presents facts** in a **clear** and **logical** manner. The purpose of a report is to offer the reader **key information** on a topic or subject. **Simplicity** and **clarity** are the necessary qualities of a good report. The **tone** is always **detached** and the **point of view** is **objective**. Reports should reach **fair conclusions,** based on the **logical** or **reasonable consequences** of their findings.

Think of the report written by the referee of an All-Ireland hurling final or an account of a road traffic accident given by a Guard in court. These documents are typical of the accurate and balanced style required for good report writing.

Reports give **clear** and **fair analysis** of **facts**.

When you write a report, use the following **five headings** to give **structure** to your writing:

1. **Terms of reference:** What is the **purpose** of the report?
2. **Procedure: How** the **information** was **gathered** and **analysed.**
3. **Findings:** The **data** or **facts** presented in the report.
4. **Conclusions:** The **logical result** arrived at in the course of the report.
5. **Recommendations:** Suggested **steps to be taken** on the basis of the conclusions.

---

exam Q

The transition year class in your school carried out a survey of how the students in third year spent an average of €10 pocket money per week. Based on the figures supplied below, write a report on this for your school magazine.

(30 marks)

(2002, Paper 1, Section 3, Functional Writing)

	Males	Females
Food/soft drinks	3.90	2.40
Leisure goods and services	2.70	1.90
Clothing	1.00	2.40
Personal goods	1.40	2.30
Transport	1.00	1.00

SAMPLE ANSWER

1. **Terms of reference**

   Transition-year students in St Fursey's Secondary School, Killinaskully, were asked by the parents' association to conduct a survey of the spending habits of the school's third-year students. The average pocket money was given as €10. The aim of the survey is to determine how pocket money is spent.

2. **Procedure**

   We surveyed 100 students, asking them to reply to the question: 'How much of your €10 pocket money do you spend on the following things?'
   (a) Food/soft drinks
   (b) Leisure goods and services
   (c) Clothing
   (d) Personal goods
   (e) Transport

3. **Findings**

   (a) Food and soft drinks account for most pocket money: 39 per cent in the case of males and 24 per cent in the case of females.
   (b) Leisure is the next priority for males, as they spend 27 per cent of their money in this area.
   (c) Females spend equal amounts on food and clothing: 24 per cent.
   (d) Females spend more of their disposable income than males on personal goods: 23 per cent compared to 14 per cent.
   (e) Males spend equal amounts on clothing and transport: 10 per cent.
   (f) Both males and females spend 10 per cent of their money on transport.

4. **Conclusions**

   (a) Transport is not a high priority for the third-year students.
   (b) Male students spend more than female students on food and leisure.
   (c) Female students give a higher priority to clothing and personal goods than their male counterparts.

5. **Recommendations**

   (a) Students are spending too much money on food and soft drinks. We recommend that the school promote a healthy eating week where students can learn about their dietary needs.
   (b) Too much pocket money is being spent on leisure. We recommend that the school gym be made available for students at appointed times free of charge.
   (c) We advise students to consider walking more in order to save the money they currently spend on transport.
   (d) The money saved should be given to transition-year students, whose needs are greater because of their maturity!

COMMENT

This answer deserves **high marks** for the following **reasons**:

Structure:	**Clear layout** following a **logical sequence.**
Content:	**Facts** and data are **presented** and **analysed.**
Language:	Sentences are **short** and **expressed clearly.**
Balance:	All recommendations are supported by **evidence.**

key point

- **Structure** and **tone** are vital to good reports.
- **Clearly outline** your **procedure.**
- Present **facts.**
- Reach **fair conclusions.**
- Recommendations must be **logical.**

Writing guidelines or instructions

In the Functional Writing section you may be asked to write a **set of instructions** or a **list of guidelines.** The essence of instructions is that they follow a **clear** and **logical sequence.** You must think about the **task** and make sure the points you write follow the **correct order.**

Imagine you were asked to **give directions** to someone driving from your school to your home. The instructions must begin in one location and outline **step by step** the **route** that must be taken to arrive at the correct destination.

Take ten minutes to write out the directions to your house. Try to **limit** the directions to **short sentences** and, if possible, limit the instructions to **ten points.** Each point should be **numbered** and begin with a **verb** in the **imperative** or command form. Model your directions on the sample points below:

1. **Turn** left at the main school gate, on to College Road.
2. **Drive** for half a kilometre to the Callan roundabout.
3. **Take** the first exit from the roundabout and **follow** the sign for Kells.

A **set of guidelines** resembles directions, as you are recommending a course of action or a series of **steps to be taken** in order to complete a task or fulfil certain conditions.

- **Clarity** is paramount here, so points are numbered.
- Each point is expressed as a command, in the **imperative** mode.
- Sentences are brief and **precise.**

You will be awarded high marks for writing guidelines or instructions in this style.

exam
Q

Write a list of safety guidelines to be displayed on a poster **EITHER** in your school's Science Lab **OR** in the Woodwork, Metalwork or Home Economics room. (30 marks)

(2007, Paper 1, Section 3, Functional Writing)

SAMPLE ANSWER

LABORATORY RULES FOR STUDENTS
1. **DO NOT** enter the laboratory without permission.
2. **DO NOT** use any equipment unless permitted to do so by the teacher. Ensure you know exactly what you are supposed to do. If in doubt, ask the teacher.
3. Long hair **MUST** always be tied back securely.
4. **ALWAYS** wear eye protection when instructed to do so.
5. **ALWAYS** check that the label on the bottle is **EXACTLY** the same as the material you require. If in doubt, ask the teacher.
6. **NOTHING** must be tasted or consumed in the laboratory.
7. Any substance accidentally taken into the mouth must be spat out **IMMEDIATELY** and the mouth washed out with plenty of water. The incident must be reported to the teacher.
8. Any cut, burn or other injury **MUST** be reported at once to the teacher.
9. Any chemicals spilled onto skin or clothing **MUST** be removed at once with plenty of water and the incident reported to the teacher.
10. **ALWAYS** wash your hands after practical work.

COMMENT
This is a good answer because:
● It is a **list** of ten instructions.
● Each instruction is in the **imperative**.
● All points are **clearly** expressed in **simple** terms.
● **Key words** are **emphasised** in bold and block capitals.

In addition to **diaries, letters, reviews, reports and instructions**, you could be asked to write a **short speech** or **pep talk** to be delivered to a team or group. **Speeches** are covered in the **Personal Writing** section of this book. A short speech, like all other functional writing tasks, must be written in 30 minutes, which is only half the time available for the Personal Writing section. The same principles of planning and composition apply.

Answer **either** Question 1 **or** Question 2.

You will be rewarded for:
- Well-structured answers.
- Clarity of expression.
- An appropriate tone.
- Good grammar, spelling and punctuation.

1. You are a member of your school's student council. As there are now students from a range of different nationalities attending the school, your principal has asked the council to come up with some suggestions to help your school to develop as an intercultural community.
    Write a report to be submitted by the student council to the principal, outlining your ideas.

OR

2. NASA (National Aeronautics and Space Administration) is running an international competition to send one student from Ireland on the next moon mission. You wish to enter the competition.
    The following are the competition entry requirements:
    1. Entries should be between 170 and 200 words.
    2. You should outline:
    - Your suitability for the mission.
    - Why you wish to participate in the mission.
    Complete your competition entry.

(30 marks)

(2008, Paper 1, Section 3, Functional Writing)

Answer **either** Question 1 **or** Question 2.

You will be rewarded for:
- Well-structured answers.
- Clarity of expression.
- An appropriate tone.
- Good grammar, spelling and punctuation.

1. You have been asked by the principal of your school to speak to the students preparing to take their Junior Certificate examinations in June 2010. Based on your experience of preparing for your own Junior Certificate examinations, write the text of **the talk** you would give to the students offering them guidance and encouragement.

OR

2. In Section One of this examination paper, Michael Morpurgo writes about the elements that he considers important to produce a piece of writing. Write **a letter** to the author in which you recount a time when you feel you wrote particularly well and explain what you think contributed to the success. In your letter you may, if you wish, comment on the earlier passage by Morpurgo or seek his advice as a writer.

See p.12 for Michael Morpurgo's extract.   (30 marks)

(2009, Paper 1, Section 3, Functional Writing)

4 Media Studies

Read	Revised	Recapped

aims
- To write **critical analysis** of media.
- To explore a **variety** of different media.
- To learn **technical terms** relevant to media studies.

This chapter will guide you through several aspects of the Media Studies section of your Junior Certificate Paper 1. In the Media Studies question, the skill you need to perfect is **critical analysis**. Often we confuse **facts** with opinions or bias when we are reading newspapers, watching TV or listening to an advertisement. In your Media Studies answer, be sure you are **critical** of the messages being expressed. This means you must **ask questions** about the **content** and the **way** it is communicated. The media are a vast group of different industries with extraordinary influence in the modern world. They permeate our lives in many ways and you should be prepared to address questions on new or emerging aspects of the industry.

It is most likely that you will be examined in the following media:

- Photographs.
- Advertisements.
- Newspapers.
- Cartoons.
- Television.
- Radio.

> **key point**
>
> Be **critical.** Learn to separate **fact** from **opinion**.

This section of the book gives you general guidelines for approaching analysis of these different media.

Photographs

Describing a Picture

Write an **accurate** and **objective** description of what you see in this photograph.   (40 marks)

Is the photo taken outside in **natural light** or indoors using **artificial lighting**?

State whether the photo is reproduced in **colour** or in **monochrome** (black and white).

Use **directions**, e.g. 'in the middle distance', 'to the right', etc.

Are some items only **partially shown**? Is anything cast in shadow?

A photo can be divided into three areas: the top third is **background**, the central third is **middle distance** and the bottom third is **foreground**.

The background can be **rural** (depicting natural landscape) or **urban** (showing organised human activity, such as industry).

SAMPLE ANSWER

This photo was taken out of doors in **natural light**. It is reproduced in full **colour**. In the **background** is a dark brown metal girder and beneath it smaller metal bars of a similar colour. It is the undercarriage of a vehicle like a lorry. Behind it, in the distance, I can see **green foliage**, which is blurred or out of focus.

The **foreground** shows a dusty red surface. There are pebbles and finer particles of sand. It is a dirt track.

In the **middle** of the photo to the left is a wheel. **We can see only half of the wheel in the frame.** The metal hub is a light grey-blue and there are signs of rust. **The tyre is worn and written on its side is the brand name: Firestone.**

Give precise **factual** detail.

Interiors of buildings also have interesting background features: coloured walls, windows, paintings, etc. Give precise details of background. Don't explain the meaning of items present; give the facts **objectively**.

The **middle distance** usually includes a person or thing that draws attention.

If people are present, give **details** of their gender, age and clothing.

The **foreground** of a photo is closest to the lens.

To the right of the tyre sits a child. He is leaning on his left hand and both of his legs are curled up to his right. His feet are bare and caked in mud. He is wearing dark brown trousers and a khaki t-shirt with a clean white collar. On his head, partially covering his face, is a military-style peaked cap. **The boy has dark brown skin and black hair.**

In front of him, in the **foreground** of the photo, are seventeen metal tubes. **They are spent bullet cartridges and the boy is arranging them in a row with his free right hand.** It looks as though the boy is **playing** a game with the empty shells.

Mention the **posture** of any people present. Do they stand, sit or run? Do they face the camera? Do they interact with other people? Give precise **factual** detail.

Give **precise** descriptions. It is easy to omit details we think are minor, but they can carry great meaning in a photo.

Look for **action**. Is there any contact between people or elements in the photo?

COMMENT

In this answer the student is careful to:

- Give precise detail.
- Stick to the facts.
- Include the entire photo.

This ensures the answer is accurate and **complete**. At no point does the personal opinion or bias of the writer affect the quality of the answer. For this reason, the analysis is **objective**. This student has answered the question very well.

Write a **clear** and **comprehensive** account of what you see in the photograph below.

Your answer should follow the pattern of the sample answer given for the earlier photograph.

(40 marks)

Reports and captions

The second type of question relating to photographs asks you to **supply a meaning** for the action in a photograph by writing a **caption** or a **news report**.

An example for Photograph 1 (p. 60) might read: 'Boy soldier plays during ceasefire in Honduras.' The caption must be **brief** and give the reader all **essential information**.

A **caption** is a line that identifies the subject or person in a photograph.

The inverted pyramid

A news report follows the structure of the **inverted pyramid**. The most crucial detail must appear in the first two paragraphs. Additional facts are given later in the article and any extra information is left until the end.

VITAL FACTS
Extra details
Background
Info

A news report will usually accompany a photograph and if you are asked to write a report, your **first paragraph** must answer the questions: **who?**, **what?**, **where?** and **when?**

A good report will give **clear information** on the action taking place in the photograph, without expressing strong opinions. The **crucial detail** must be communicated in the **initial paragraphs** of the report to facilitate later editing of the story, should the newspaper need to alter it quickly. **Later paragraphs** will offer **analysis** by answering the **how?** and **why?** questions, explaining the **reasons** for an event taking place and suggesting possible future **consequences**. A good news reporter will keep the report **objective** by sticking to the facts and not taking sides when telling a story.

Newspapers

Newspapers continue to be the most significant part of the print media. Most people divide newspapers into **tabloid or broadsheet**. Although the original meaning of these terms referred to the size (format) of paper used in the production of the newspaper, it also has connotations of **quality**. Broadsheet newspapers are associated with quality reporting. This means that people expect a higher level of **accuracy** and a **less emotive** style of writing. It does not always follow, however, that a tabloid article will be more **sensational** or biased than a broadsheet one, but the audience for each type of paper has come to expect a certain style in the treatment of the news. Some critics have suggested that all newspapers are becoming more sensational in their reporting of news stories because of the pressure of increased competition.

1. The first task in analysing a report is to determine the **accuracy of the factual content**. Does the reporter give the vital information?

2. Secondly, is the report fair and balanced or does it reflect some **bias** on the writer's part? The reader expects an objective account that gives a comprehensive range of information, allowing us to arrive at our own judgement of the events.

3. The third step is to examine the nature of the language used. If the writer uses **emotive language**, there will be vocabulary that tries to evoke a strong emotional reaction from the audience, rather than a cool rational response. We must always be alert to the possibility that the writer is manipulating us by using emotionally biased language.

4. It is always useful to ask who the **target audience** for a report is. Does it appeal to a general readership? Does it require specialist knowledge? Does the jargon used suggest a particular age profile for the intended readers?

5. Be **critical**. Too often we adopt a very trusting approach to stories that appear in the media. If you read carefully, you become aware of underlying assumptions being made in news reports. A good critical analysis will require you to give a strong, **independent opinion** of the **quality** of an article.

6. You should always support your response with **evidence** from the article. The verbal and visual components, including headlines and sub-headlines, are all useful in this regard. Your answer should attempt to explain or interpret any quotation or reference from the text.

exam Q   **A**   **Read the article below and answer the questions that follow.**

Sunday Tribune
28 June 2009

BRIGHTEST STAR GOES OUT IN THE CITY OF ANGELS

By Mark Hilliard

Crowds surrounded the UCLA Medical Center – where Michael Jackson died last Thursday afternoon – despite appeals to the contrary. They were also forced back from the entrance to his mansion above Sunset Boulevard.

A confluence of mourners, ordinary fans, young and old, converged on Hollywood Boulevard with its bright lights, glitz and commercial insignia, the same that had surrounded Jackson since childhood. Perhaps this pavement strip of dedicated stars, as a focal point of farewell, seemed strange; but it was certainly fitting.

'It is not uncommon for people here to pay their respects at a star on Hollywood Boulevard if they have nowhere else to go,' explained Mary Catherine O'Sullivan, an LA resident amongst the lines of admirers and curious passers-by.

Bouquets of flowers, photographs and messages of love adorned the patio surrounded by steel fencing and police officers. If it were possible anywhere in the world to avoid news that the 'king of pop' had passed away, LA was certainly not the place. Driving down its freeways, queuing in supermarkets, eating lunch in the sun-bleached boulevards – there was little else on people's lips.

And it stands to reason. This was the state where Michael Jackson had forged his reputation: as a performer and as an eccentric loner in the surreal Neverland estate where life stood at a standstill.

It is where he had furthered a career that spanned decades and made him the most revered performer in the history of modern entertainment.

It was also the location where the 50-year-old was putting the final touches to a sensational comeback tour, designed not only to settle debts of hundreds of millions of dollars but also to reconcile an often enigmatic musician with a global audience he had long since divorced. Jackson had not toured since 1997; his last album was in 2001.

From early on Thursday the airwaves and television channels flashed seemingly endless pictures of a lifetime of performance. Friends and colleagues filled the national airwaves with tributes and similar tales of disbelief and sadness.

And in the news reporting there was an undercurrent of mystery and drama, even conspiracy. The story unfolded by the minute, each word, comment and development flooding through car radios and network bulletins.

Jackson, who had a cardiac arrest at his rented Holmby Hills mansion above Sunset Boulevard, was pronounced dead at the university medical centre at 2.26p.m. on Thursday. When his autopsy was completed at lunchtime the following day, throngs of reporters gathered to hear the results. A delay in pronouncing an official cause of death will continue to add spice to the final chapter of a remarkable story.

There were questions surrounding what medication he may have been on. Where was his personal doctor, whose car had been taken away by the police? When would his body be released to his family? Were extra security precautions being taken to guard it? Most questions remained unanswered. What was certain, though, was that in death, as in life, Jackson's global appeal is undisputed.

'People fell to their knees,' Kenny Ortega, his concert director for a run of upcoming London shows, told the *Los Angeles Times*.

Those concerts, and a much-anticipated three-year comeback tour, will now, of course, never happen.

Until the final curtain, Jackson had kept his legions of loyal fans guessing, but in the end his dramatic and final performance was one of simple tragedy.

Questions

1. What vital pieces of information are revealed in the first two paragraphs?
   (10 marks)
2. How well does the writer introduce details of the background to this Michael Jackson story?
   (10 marks)
3. Is this a tabloid- or broadsheet-style report? Explain your answer with reference to the text of the article.
   (20 marks)

Hints

The **first question** is a very precise one. You must limit your answer to include only information in the first and second paragraphs. Think of the following prompts:

- Who is the story about?
- What happened?
- Where did it take place?
- When did this event happen?

The **second question** requires more analysis from you. In a well-written news report, the inverted pyramid structure means that background detail is given in the middle or towards the end of the story. A good writer will find a way to **link** the relevant back story to more recent events. Read carefully to see **how** Mark Hilliard **introduces these details** and comment on the effectiveness of his writing.

The **third question** carries 20 marks, compared to questions 1 and 2, which are worth 10 marks each. For this reason, you should **divide your time** accordingly. The final question requires you to identify the qualities of tabloid- or broadsheet-style reporting present in this piece of writing. Think about the following:

- Is the subject matter of the story, fans mourning the death of a celebrity, more typical of tabloid or broadsheet newspaper coverage?
- Does the article report a good balance of facts and well-supported opinion? Tabloid style is usually associated with exaggeration and hyperbole.
- What is the quality of the language used? If the writer uses emotive language, it is more likely to be a tabloid-style story.

Beware of **bias** in the media! Bias is when only **one side** of a story is being told.

B   **Read the article from *The Sun* newspaper below and answer the questions that follow.**

The Sun
20 November 2009

HENRY'S £1BN CASH IN HAND

By Nick Parker

Thierry Henry yesterday apologised for the handball that helped France beat Ireland to reach the World Cup finals. He said in a 'tweet' on his Twitter website: 'I'm not the referee – but if I hurt someone I'm sorry.'

> **twitter**   Home Profile Find People Settings Help Sign out
>
> im not the referee... but if i hurt some one im sorry
> 10:28 AM Nov 19th from web
> Retweeted by 100+ people   Reply Retweet
>
> Thierry_Henry
> Thierry Henry

So sorry ... Henry's apology for handball on his Twitter page.

Yet the 32-year-old former Arsenal ace had earlier spoken proudly about laying on the extra-time goal for pal William Gallas – claiming that it was destiny and that the strike would go down in **HISTORY**.

Last night economists said reaching next summer's World Cup extravaganza in South Africa was worth **£1BILLION** to a nation the size of France.

Paris-dona ... Henry handles before French winner.

Simon Chadwick, professor of sports business strategy at Coventry University, said: 'There will be a ripple-out effect into areas that are directly related, such as sports betting and magazine publishing.

'But it will ripple out even further to electronics retailers and manufacturers, because people tend to buy more televisions around tournaments too. It's a psychological issue – sporting success makes people feel more optimistic generally and predisposed to buying.'

Punters in France – motto Liberté, Egalité, Fraternité – will also pour money into kits, sticker albums, tickets and travel, he said.

Chris Brady, Dean of BPP Business School, said: 'France will get a boost around the tournament, with extra sales of some goods and people flying in and out of the country.

'There's also the general feelgood factor to an economy of people just feeling better – better morale.'

Meanwhile Ireland's economy, already mired in the deepest recession in Europe, will **LOSE** out on about £100 million, experts warned.

Financial analyst Owen James, of London's prestigious Centre for Economics and Business Research, said: 'Based on figures on household expenditure and other factors I estimate the Irish economy will lose out to the tune of £100 million.

'If they'd got beyond the group stage, the gain would be more.'

Henk Potts, of Barclays Stockbrokers, said: 'Retailers will lose out in terms of numbers of sales, and the leisure industry in terms of the numbers going to pubs and bars. Supermarkets would have expected an increase in certain products sold in preparation for matches and bookmakers would expect a lot more activity if Ireland were taking part.'

Ruth Lea, former governor of the London School of Economics, said: 'The French don't need this boost like the Irish do and they don't deserve it because they cheated.

'Psychologically and economically, qualifying would have been far more important to Ireland.'

Gallas's killer goal came after the Irish

Maradona ... Hand of God goal v England in 1986.

had battled through 1,004 minutes of World Cup qualifiers.

The team, led by skipper Robbie Keane, lost the first leg of their play-off with France last weekend.

But they levelled the aggregate score in Paris on Wednesday night to take the tie into extra time.

And they were beaten only after Henry controlled the ball with his hand before crossing for team-mate Gallas to nudge home.

The jubilant teammates hugged each other as they celebrated at the final whistle.

Defeated ... Irish skipper Robbie Keane.

And Henry said after the game: 'You know, I've known William for a long time.

'I don't want to turn it into a night of nostalgia, but we went to school together, we have the same birthday, we went to the Clairefontaine academy together. The fact I managed to pick out William was a great moment. It will go down in history.'

The incident, which echoed Diego Maradona's infamous 'Hand of God' goal against England, sparked a furious response from observers, including Ireland legends Niall Quinn and Liam Brady.

Irish PM Brian Cowen is set to discuss it with French President Nicolas Sarkozy at an EU summit.

A spokeswoman for the Taoiseach said: 'He was asked if he was planning on raising the matter with President Sarkozy and he said he wouldn't, but he will mention it in person when they meet.'

Cowen fumed: 'I think that fair play is a fundamental part of the game.'

© *The Sun* 20th November 2009/nisyndication.com

Questions

1. According to this article, what are the economic consequences of qualifying for the World Cup finals? (10 marks)
2. What evidence of bias can you find in this report? (10 marks)
3. Write a short dialogue between Brian Cowen and Nicholas Sarkozy, where they discuss the match in question. (20 marks)

exam focus

Spend no longer than **30 minutes** on your Media Studies question.

Analysing an advertisment

Pictures, photographs and other graphic elements such as logos are often used as visual elements in advertisements. Very many Media Studies questions focus on advertising. It is important to remember that all advertising is a form of **persuasion**. The techniques used to communicate a commercial message frequently involve the **distortion of reality** or **exaggeration** in order to sell the product. There are several tried and tested techniques advertisers employ to get their message across. Some of these methods relate to the use of **visual** elements in the presentation and other strategies involve tricks with **language**. In order to discuss advertising, it is useful to consider **four** aspects of this branch of the media: **representation**, **product or service**, **audience** and **techniques of persuasion**.

Representation

Every advertisement offers us a view of the world that is **biased** in some way. Cosmetics commercials usually show close-up photographs of glamorous models in their teens or early twenties whose complexion is improved by tricks such as airbrushing. Advertisements for cars often show a motorist driving along an empty stretch of road in a picturesque landscape, hardly ever stuck in a traffic jam in a cloud of exhaust fumes!

You should always pay attention to the way adverts can exaggerate and offer a **stereotyped** image of certain groups of people. Ask yourself who is being shown or represented in the graphic. Does the picture give a false message about gender, race, age or families? If there is a **distortion**, then **why** has the advertiser chosen to exaggerate certain features of this group?

In the advertisement for Nissan X-Trail, a young couple is featured. The man is shown snowboarding on a mountainside, while the woman shops on the high street. Clearly the commercial is inviting us to accept a very extreme view of the differences between young men and young women. The assumption is that all young men choose to engage in adventure sports, while all young women spend their free time buying clothes.

key point

Ask yourself **who** is represented in an advertisement and **why** this is so.

Product or service

Every advertisement attempts to **convince us** of the benefits of a product or service. Some public service messages present us with useful information or warn us of certain hazards that we should avoid. We are all familiar with television advertisements that discourage underage drinking, binge drinking and drink driving. Whatever the specific message, every advertisement aims to **change our behaviour** in some way.

Analysis of an advertisement must focus on the product or service at the heart of the message:

- **Identify** the product. It will usually be named several times, often with a picture of a typical consumer using it.
- Pay attention to the **location** of the product. Most advertisements will highlight it by placing it in the foreground of the picture.
- For certain products, the **camera angle** is important, as it will show the product in the most flattering way.

Look again at the Nissan X-Trail advertisement. The angle allows us to view the front and the side of the car simultaneously. The photographer chose a **low angle shot** to emphasise the size and power of the vehicle. As in many advertisements, the **colour** of the product is echoed in the background and other details. The **logo** appears prominently on the front grille and this links with the strategic placing of the logo in the bottom right-hand corner. A further connection is established between the **copy** (text) and the **graphic** (photo) by the number plate, which identifies the car as 'X-Trail'.

Your analysis could concentrate on how the product is being used or how the service is being presented. Usually the advertisement will adopt **emotive** techniques to convince us that our feeling of wellbeing or happiness will be guaranteed if we purchase the item being sold.

key point

Emotive advertising appeals to our feelings, not our reason.

Audience

Every advertisement is aimed at a target audience. This is a group determined by age, gender and disposable income. The advertiser will set out to attract a particular group, as these are the potential customers for the company's product. Most advertisements will give us a **visual representation** of a **typical consumer**, but often there are **verbal clues** in the copy that help to identify the audience being addressed.

The Nissan ad shows a man in the 20–35 age group. It also shows the arm of a woman of similar age. The commercial links them as a couple and no children or other family members are shown. The copy tells us that prices range from €31,225 to €36,225, which limits the target audience to those who can afford the expense of this vehicle. Finally, the copy promises 'a new spirit of adventure in the heart of the city', hinting that the car is aimed at urban consumers.

Techniques of persuasion

Advertising agencies are highly skilled in the art of persuasion. There are several tried and tested strategies they employ to lure the consumer into purchasing a product or service. Some of these methods are outlined below:

1. **Emotive language and symbolism**
   Words or pictures are used to elicit a powerful feeling in the reader. By **appealing to our emotions** advertisers hope we will overlook the exaggerated claims they make for their product and buy it on impulse. A recent advertisement for Lynx deodorant includes the slogan: *Spray More to Get More!* The clear implication is that your prospects of romantic success increase as you use this product.

2. **Repetition**
   Words or phrases are used **repeatedly**. This helps to lodge the product securely in the consumer's mind, e.g. *Brennans – Today's Bread Today!*

3. **Rhyme**
   This works like a **radio jingle**, establishing the brand in the consumer's mind, e.g. *Grace. . . Space. . . Pace* (Jaguar Cars).

4. **Humour**
   Carlsberg commercials use humour relating to the slogans: *Carlsberg don't do...* and *Probably the best lager in the world*. Each advertisement explores a comical fantasy world.

5. **Glamour**
   The product is associated with a lifestyle of prestige, success or beauty. In the Nissan advertisement on p. 69, it is implied that Nissan drivers snowboard in the Alps and shop in expensive boutiques on Grafton Street!

6. **Superlative adjectives**
   Features are described in the **superlative** to suggest that the product is the ultimate in terms of quality, e.g. *Simply the Best!* (*RTÉ Guide*).

7. **Imperative verbs**
   Verbs are used in the imperative to convey **urgency** and to create a sense of necessity in buying the product. The most famous advertising command is Nike's *Just do it*.

8. Slogans

Memorable short phrases, often repeated in the course of an advertisement. Examples include: *Pleasure you can't measure* (Mars Delight); and *Shift expectations* (Nissan).

9. Logos

Symbols used to represent the company, brand or organisation. Often they are more effective than language, because they can be recognised by all nationalities and they have greater power to evoke emotion from the audience. The most internationally recognisable logos include: the McDonald's golden arch; the Mercedes Benz star; and the Nike tick.

10. Colour

The colour scheme usually ties in with the product or with prominent colours in the company logo. Notice how the Nissan X-Trail advertisement on p. 69 uses cool blues and silver repeatedly: on the surface of the roadway, on the shopping bag, on the man's hat and in the sky.

11. Buzz words

The following buzz words appear in the Nissan X-Trail advertisement on p. 69: perfect, amazing, satisfy, choice, only, more, new, adventure and heart. They are chosen because they inspire positive feelings.

12. Endorsement

This is when a celebrity is shown using the product, to encourage others to buy it, e.g. Roger Federer for Rolex and Eva Longoria for Magnum ice-cream.

If you are asked to write a critical analysis of an advertisement, you will find some of this terminology useful.

The steps outlined below will help to give focus to your analysis:

1. Your analysis should **identify the product** or service.
2. Ask yourself what the advertisement is **promising** the consumer. Is the product being linked to increased popularity, greater health, a sense of security, a glamorous lifestyle, an exciting social life?
3. Now try to determine **how** these emotions are being elicited. Which key words or phrases are most effective? Is there a link between the words and the images used? What connections are suggested between the product or service and a pleasant experience for the customer?
4. How does the advertisement **exaggerate** aspects of the real world? Are there examples of gender or racial stereotyping?
5. Who are the **target audience**? Are they individuals grouped by age, gender or social class? Does the advertisement appeal to different groups at the same time, e.g. young parents, small children, older people, students or couples?

The **target audience** is the specific group of people the advert is addressing.

C **Look carefully at the advertisement below for Iarnród Éireann and answer the questions that follow.**

1. What message does this public service advertisement express?
   (10 marks)
2. Describe the target audience for this advertisement.
   (10 marks)
3. What links can be made between the copy (text) and the graphic (photograph)?
   (10 marks)
4. Do you think this is a good piece of advertising for Iarnród Éireann? Explain your answer.
   (10 marks)

Common Courtesy-Pass It On!
Help Us To Help You.

Our staff are committed to assisting you with your travel arrangements in a courteous and helpful manner.

We are also committed to providing a safe work environment for our staff.

Where staff are subjected to offensive, violent or threatening behaviour while carrying out their duties, we will not hesitate to take appropriate action. (As provided for in the Iarnród Éireann Bye-laws)

Thank you for your co-operation.

irishrail.ie   Iarnród Éireann

Cartoons

Many newspapers regularly feature cartoons. Cartoons are a form of graphic humour and encapsulate a view of news, or some aspect of life, in a **concise** way. A cartoon can convey more in one frame (or several frames in the case of a cartoon strip) than many pages of text. In early 2006, a single-frame cartoon in a Danish newspaper gave rise to controversy over its portrayal of the prophet Muhammad. Subsequent demonstrations led to many deaths around the world. Cartoons are probably the only aspect of the media that are truly **international** in their appeal and effectiveness, since cartoons are more visual than verbal and are accessible to many nationalities.

The power of a cartoon to lampoon or satirise its target can also lead to a polarisation of responses from different audiences. Overtly **political** cartoons have been used to criticise governments and politicians of all persuasions. Less controversial are the cartoons that make fun of **common human foolishness**. Either way, cartoons are an art form and a popular aspect of the print media. Animated cartoons are also a very successful element of television programming.

The analysis of a cartoon involves many of the same steps used for analysing advertisements. There are usually both **visual and verbal** elements. The cartoon seeks to exaggerate some comical detail. Sometimes, cartoons offer a **caricature** or stereotype of individuals or groups, by taking a perceived **trait** and highlighting it above other aspects of the subject. In reviewing cartoons, you should be alert to this hyperbole or exaggeration.

It is also worth asking **why** a message in a particular cartoon is more powerful than a serious article of a thousand words on the same subject. Good cartoons appeal to both the head and the heart, evoking a powerful range of feelings and sometimes arousing several conflicting emotions.

Consider whether the cartoon appeals to a particular **audience**. Like all other media, there is a deliberate targeting of specific groups and this can be discerned by looking at the **style** and **content** of the cartoon. Many overtly political cartoons are aimed at an adult audience, while cartoon strips featuring children are often produced with a younger viewer in mind.

D Look at the cartoon and answer the questions that follow.

1. Explain in 30 words the message in this cartoon. **(10 marks)**

2. Who is the cartoon making fun of? Explain your answer. **(10 marks)**

3. What is unique about cartoons as a form? **(20 marks)**

Radio

Radio is the form of mass media that relies exclusively on **sound** to communicate with its audience. Irish people have access to: local radio stations; national broadcasters, such as RTÉ and Today FM; and now, through the Internet, international stations like the BBC World Service. Recent exam questions have focused on radio programming and why radio is still such a popular form of media.

Radio programmes and stations are broadly divided between: **talk radio**, which tends to focus on news, current affairs and public access or phone-in shows; and **music stations**, where talk is kept to a minimum.

It is useful to consider **target audience** when you are asked a question about radio stations or programmes. Music stations can be grouped according to genre, e.g. Lyric FM is a classical music station, while 2FM broadcasts rock and pop music. Certain music genres are aimed at certain **age profiles**. Pop music tends to be popular with pre-teens, teens and young adults. Other genres may have different appeal.

Talk radio is extremely popular in Ireland, both at local and national levels. Irish people love good storytelling and radio offers people a perfect opportunity to tell their story or indeed to listen to others tell theirs.

Irish radio also has a strong tradition of comedy or satire, where public figures like celebrities or politicians are made fun of on spoof radio shows. *Scrap Saturday*, 'Nob Nation' and 'Gift Grub' are popular examples of this type of radio broadcasting.

 E Read the article below and answer the question that follows.

The Irish Times
9 May 2009

'GIFT GRUB' RADIO TEAM MARK 10-YEAR ANNIVERSARY OF DISHING OUT THE SATIRE

By Ronan McGreevy

Ten years ago this week, the *Ian Dempsey Breakfast Show* on Today FM tried out a new comedy sketch called 'Gift Grub'.

It was supposed to be a light-hearted take on a populist taoiseach, Bertie Ahern, cooking up a few of his own recipes. 'I thought we'd run out of ideas after three months,' recalls the show's ever-present writer and performer Mario Rosenstock.

'Gift Grub' did its bit in cementing Bertie's reputation as a self-styled man-of-the-people with his pints of Bass, his love of 'Man U' and his fruity choice of language, mostly notably his repeated use of the words 'spanner' and 'Jaysus'.

Yesterday morning, the real former taoiseach rang up the show to congratulate the 'Gift Grub' team on their tenth anniversary. He had not heard the programme in the early days, but 'never got further than the corridor' of Government Buildings before somebody appraised him of its contents.

'It has been terrific fun. It was never vindictive. Not since Dermot Morgan and *Scrap Saturday* has there been a programme that has had such good satire,' he said. The real Bertie confessed to using 'Jaysus' once or twice, 'but I shouldn't be taking the Lord's name,' he said.

He attributed the comedy's success to the versatility of the sketches. 'There was something in it for everybody. It was not just about politics.'

Rosenstock said he was particularly proud that Gift Grub listeners picked 160 different sketches as their favourite. 'I was just saying to Ian [Dempsey] that it really lights up your day when you hear these stories of people laughing in cars and looking across to each other and they are both laughing at the same time.'

Rosenstock singles out his encounter with the real Roy Keane and José Mourinho as two of his favourite highlights. Mourinho was so impressed with Rosenstock's note-perfect mimicry, particularly on the single 'José and his Amazing Technicolour Overcoat', that he invited Rosenstock to Chelsea. Rosenstock's Mourinho lives on as a puppet on Setanta Sports.

The Best of Gift Grub has become a perennial bestselling CD. Catchphrases such as Bertie Ahern's 'spanner' and 'all credit to' (as attributed to Roy Keane), along with Enda Kenny's 'love of Lilt' are as well-known as anything the characters themselves do in real life. And Rosenstock conceded that he could be criticised for not being harder on the former taoiseach when he was in office.

exam focus

Think about your **favourite** radio show or station and identify **why** you like to listen to it.

Question

1. Write a short proposal (100 words) for Mario Rosenstock, where you suggest a new celebrity character for 'Gift Grub'. Your answer should include:
    *   The name of the celebrity.
    *   Aspects of his/her character that have comic potential.
    *   Possible storylines involving this new 'Gift Grub' character.   (40 marks)

Television

Television revolutionised mass media in the twentieth century. It has immense power and influence in our lives, as audiences grow and the number of hours we spend viewing continues to rise.

Critical analysis of television will force you to draw on your **own knowledge and use** of the medium. You should keep in mind the points made earlier in this chapter about **audience, representation, product** and **techniques of persuasion** (see p. 71). Television employs all of these strategies and it is important to **question** the messages we receive about the world from television programmes.

Television audiences are notoriously **fickle**. People follow trends, as the producers of programmes decide which forms of entertainment to promote through the medium. Game shows, soap operas, situation comedies and reality shows have all proved immensely popular at different times.

While entertainment is important, television can also be used to inform or **educate** us about the world around us. News programmes and documentaries are valuable ways to highlight serious issues. In 2009, the parents of Madeleine McCann made a short TV advertisement which was aimed at keeping pressure on her abductors by appealing to the conscience of their family and friends. Television is the most effective way to reach a **mass audience** with an urgent message.

 F **Read the article below and answer the questions that follow.**

Guardian
16 December 2009

ITV1 DOMINATES LIST OF 2009'S MOST-WATCHED TV SHOWS

By Tara Conlan

ITV1 is set to claim the 2009 ratings crown, with the *Britain's Got Talent* final proving the most popular show of the year and the broadcaster airing six of the top 10 most-watched programmes up to early December.

BBC1 will be hoping for strong figures for *EastEnders* and *Doctor Who* on Christmas Day, but neither is likely to overhaul the 18.3 million viewers who watched the final of the third series of *Britain's Got Talent* on 30 May, a 68 per cent audience share, as the dance group Diversity beat Susan Boyle.

The *Britain's Got Talent* final was the highest-rating programme on any UK channel since 20 June 2006, when 18.5 million watched England v Sweden in the 2006 World Cup.

ITV1 had six out of the top 10 programmes on any channel this year, according to figures provided by the broadcaster up to 29 November.

The X Factor results show on 15 November took second place with 15 million viewers, although that will be replaced in the final end-of-year list by the ITV1 talent show's final last Sunday, which had an average live audience of 15.5 million viewers over two hours. This figure will go up when timeshifted viewing – including on video recorders and personal video recorders such as Sky+ – is added by ratings body Barb.

An episode of *EastEnders* on 2 April was BBC1's most popular show, gathering 11.457 million viewers and a 49 per cent audience share. ITV1's *Coronation Street* on 2 February was just behind with 11.456 million viewers and a 41 per cent share.

The highest-rated non-soap drama was ITV1's Martin Clunes vehicle *Doc Martin* on 8 November, with 10.3 million viewers tuning in. *Strictly Come Dancing* was BBC1's most popular entertainment show, closely followed by last month's *Children in Need*, both with just over 10 million viewers. ITV1 also looks set to dominate the drama top 10 in 2009, with the channel taking six of the top 10 spots and *Doc Martin* topping the bill.

BBC1's *Doctor Who* took second place with 9.9 million viewers for last month's special 'The Waters of Mars', and an episode of *Jonathan Creek* broadcast on New Year's Day was in third place.

But ITV1 can take heart from its new Rupert Penry-Jones drama *Whitechapel*, with 9.2 million viewers, taking fourth place. And regular ratings-winner *Wild at Heart* continued to prove popular, scooping sixth place in the drama list with 8.5 million. Most promisingly for ITV1, the network aired the top seven new dramas on any channel this year.

Charity shows did well for BBC1 this year, winning four of the top 10 entertainment shows spots. They included *Kilimanjaro: The Big Red Nose Climb*, which drew 9.2 million, and *Comic Relief Does the Apprentice*, which scored 8.5 million.

The BBC won the top spot in the top 10 sports programmes of the year, with the Wimbledon tennis finals pulling in 8.5 million viewers.

There was also some good news for Katie Price and Peter Andre, as their various shows on ITV2 accounted for four of the top 10 most popular multichannel programmes of the year. The most popular of the Peter and Katie outings was *Peter Andre: Going It Alone*, which won 2.2 million viewers and a 12 per cent multichannel share on 17 August.

The highest-rated multichannel show of 2009 was an edition of *The Xtra Factor* results show on ITV2 on 8 November, with 2.78 million viewers.

Questions

1. What genre of programmes was most popular in the UK in 2009? (10 marks)

2. Explain why you think so many people watch programmes like *Britain's Got Talent*, *The X Factor* and *Strictly Come Dancing*? (10 marks)

3. Describe your favourite TV programme and explain its particular appeal for you. (20 marks)

Answer **either** Question 1 **or** Question 2.

1. Look at the advertisement for RTÉ 2FM below.

   (a) Based on your reading of the advertisement, identify the target audience it is aimed at and explain how you arrived at this conclusion. You must refer to the advertisement in your answer. (20 marks)

   (b) There is a perception that many young people only want to listen to music-based radio. Based on your experience of Media Studies, what do you think would make talk radio more attractive to young people? (20 marks)

OR

2. Look at the information about the on-screen classification of television programmes below.

(a) Explain fully the term watershed as it applies to the on-screen classification system. (10 marks)

(b) Explain what kinds of programmes can be shown before the watershed. (10 marks)

(c) Give reasons why you do or do not think that the classification system is a good idea. (20 marks)

GA | **General Audience (GA)**
a programme that would be acceptable to all ages and tastes.

Ch | **Children (Ch)**
a programme aimed specifically at children, pre-teenage or a very young teenage audience.

YA | **Young Adult (YA)**
a programme aimed at a teenage audience.

PS | **Parental Supervision (PS)**
a programme aimed at a mature audience.

MA | **Mature Audience (MA)**
a typical 'post-watershed' programme.

(2009, Paper 1, Section 4, Media Studies)

The **Media Studies** question is the **last** question on **Paper 1**. It carries **40 marks** out of 180 for Paper 1. Spend no longer than **30 minutes** on it.

Paper 2

5 Drama

Read	Revised	Recapped

aims

- To identify **features** of drama.
- To learn about **Shakespearean** and **non-Shakespearean** drama.
- To analyse elements of **stagecraft**.
- To understand the **structure** of drama answers.

Junior Certificate English Paper 2 starts with the Drama questions. You must attempt **one Unseen Drama** question and **one Studied Drama** question.

Unseen drama

The Unseen Drama section is divided into **two options:**

- **Shakespearean** drama
  or
- **Other** drama.

exam focus

The **Unseen Drama** and **Studied Drama** questions carry equal marks: **30 marks each**.

exam focus

Studying a Shakespeare play in class is excellent preparation for the **Unseen Shakespeare** option.

Shakespearean drama

When you write about a play, the following elements are important, as they combine in any production of the play to make the words on the page come alive on stage in front of an audience. The skills required to produce a good play are referred to as **stagecraft**.

Language

If you have already studied a play by William Shakespeare, then you may feel confident about answering the Unseen Shakespeare question. Do not be put off by the **Elizabethan style** of English. Since you have already read and studied a play by Shakespeare, you know that it is not essential to understand the precise meaning of every word in order to make sense of a scene. Any **obscure** or **archaic** words will be explained in a brief **glossary**.

Genre

Shakespeare's plays fall into **three main categories**:

- **Tragedies**.
- **Comedies**.
- **Historical** dramas.

Often they explore events of great importance, like battles or the death of a king. For this reason, the **dramatic quality** of the story is usually quite striking. There is typically a strong **contrast** between characters, which makes it easier to discuss the personality and emotions of each individual.

Themes

Shakespeare's themes are **universal**: love, revenge, justice, jealousy, rivalry, betrayal, war, marriage and family. The universal nature of the themes suggests that the Unseen Shakespeare question is an option you should seriously consider.

Character

The chosen passage is always **short** and focused on a **key moment** in the play. Read the questions **carefully** and underline or **highlight** the **key words**. When you read the passage, remember that the **background paragraph** provided will always contain valuable information. It will give you useful **clues** about the meaning of the scene. You may **quote** from this in one or more of your answers. Underline **key words in the dialogue** as you read.

    If a question focuses on **one particular character**, you should pay attention to:

- What **they say**.
- What **others say** about them.
- **Actions** they perform while on stage.

The **text in *italics*** is referred to as **stage directions** and it gives us some idea of when and how action happens. Sometimes the stage directions even reveal how a character is **feeling** at a particular moment.

Costume, make-up and props

A question about a character may also ask you to make suggestions about **how** he or she should **appear on stage**. Look closely at the

dialogue for **clues** about how the character is **dressed,** so that you can recommend an appropriate **costume.** Some characters may require special **make-up** to exaggerate certain aspects of their physical appearance. If **props** are mentioned, you should refer to them and explain how the character uses them.

Voice, movement and posture

Character is expressed through **voice**. Consider each of the following:

- **Tone** of voice.
- **Volume**.
- **Pace**.

Meaning is also expressed through **the body**. Consider:

- **Posture** or stance.
- **Gestures**.
- **Movement**.

Each of these elements is important in conveying the **meaning** of the lines of dialogue. If you mention that an actor should perform a particular gesture, then you should support this idea by referring to the **relevant lines** in the dialogue.

Actors are performing even when they are not speaking, so it is important to think about **how the people on the stage are responding to the words and actions of others**. The stage directions tell you who is on stage and who enters or leaves during the scene. As words are spoken, ask yourself:

- **Who is on stage** at this moment?
- **What is each character doing**?

Lighting

When you imagine a scene on stage, think about how lights can be used to **focus the attention** of the audience. Lighting also establishes certain **moods** or feelings, mainly through the use of **colour** and shadow.

Set

The **design** of a **backdrop** for the play (furniture, walls, doorways, etc.) is important in setting the scene. Some Unseen questions invite you to make suggestions about how **you** would use these elements to **stage the scene**.

Focused **knowledge** of **stagecraft** will earn you high marks in the exam.

A Read this extract from Act I, Scene 2 of *Henry V* by William Shakespeare and answer the questions that follow. Guidelines are given at the end of the questions to indicate how you should approach your answers.

Background to the extract

King Henry has just ascended to the throne of England. During his youth, he spent some time in France and enjoyed sport, dancing and going to parties. Now that he has inherited the crown, he must devote himself to more serious issues. His political advisers have told him that he has a justifiable claim to the kingdom of France. In this scene King Henry meets with an ambassador for the Dauphin. The Dauphin is the eldest son of the French king and heir to the throne, according to French claims.

King Henry V
William Shakespeare

KING HENRY:	Call in the messengers sent from the Dauphin[1].
	Exeunt some attendants
	Now are we well resolv'd; and, by God's help
	And yours, the noble sinews of our power,
	France being ours, we'll bend it to our awe,
	Or break it all to pieces!
	Enter ambassadors of France
	Now are we well prepar'd to know the pleasure
	Of our fair cousin Dauphin.
AMBASSADOR:	Your Highness, lately sending into France,
	Did claim some certain dukedoms in the right
	Of your great predecessor, King Edward the Third.
	In answer of which claim, the Prince our master

	Says that you savour too much of your youth,

Says that you savour too much of your youth,
And bids you be advis'd there's nought in France
That can be with a nimble galliard[2] won;
You cannot revel[3] into dukedoms there.
He therefore sends you, meeter[4] for your spirit,
This tun[5] of treasure; and, in lieu of this,
Desires you let the dukedoms that you claim
Hear no more of you. This the Dauphin speaks.

KING HENRY: What treasure, uncle?

EXETER: Tennis-balls, my liege.

KING HENRY: We are glad the Dauphin is so pleasant with us;
His present and your pains we thank you for.
When we have match'd our rackets to these balls,
We will in France, by God's grace, play a set
Shall strike his father's crown into the hazard[6].
And we understand him well,
How he comes o'er us with our wilder days,
Not measuring what use we made of them.
But tell the Dauphin I will keep my state,
Be like a king, and show my sail of greatness,
When I do rouse me in my throne of France;
And tell the pleasant Prince this mock of his
Hath turn'd his balls to gun-stones, and his soul
Shall stand sore charged for the wasteful vengeance
That shall fly with them; for many a thousand widows
Shall this his mock mock out of their dear husbands;
Mock mothers from their sons, mock castles down;
And some are yet ungotten and unborn
That shall have cause to curse the Dauphin's scorn.
So get you hence in peace; and tell the Dauphin
His jest will savour but of shallow wit,
When thousands weep more than did laugh at it.
Convey them with safe conduct. Fare you well.
Exeunt ambassadors

1. Dauphin: French prince
2. nimble galliard: lively dancing
3. revel: party
4. meeter: more suitable
5. tun: cask
6. hazard: danger or part of a tennis court, scores in tennis

Questions

1. King Henry is insulted by the message he receives from the Dauphin. Why is he so upset? (10 marks)
2. If you were directing the actors in this scene, what advice would you give to the actor playing King Henry about how to deliver his speeches here? (10 marks)
3. Imagine the scene where the Ambassador returns to France. Write the dialogue between the Ambassador and his master the Dauphin. (10 marks)

Hints for approaching these questions

1. The first question asks you to **identify why** the King feels **insulted** by the Dauphin. The Dauphin has sent both a **verbal message** through his ambassador and a **physical gift**. King Henry is **insulted by the words** of the Dauphin and by the **gift of a 'tun' of tennis balls**.

   In your answer, you should pinpoint the **precise words** that so offended King Henry. Your second paragraph will link these words to the 'gift' of the tennis balls. Look again at the background to the extract for further clues as to **why** this present combined with the words of the message would have **angered** the new king at this time.

   Finally, you should give some thought to the fact that the **Dauphin is a prince**, while the man he is communicating with is a **king**. The difference between their respective ranks is also relevant to this question.

2. Answering the second question requires you to have a good grasp of the **character** of King Henry. We know from the background information that he is a **new ruler** whose **reputation** for the playboy lifestyle of his youth may be a source of embarrassment to him. The introduction also reveals a man under some **pressure** to claim authority over a 'foreign' land.

   His initial lines, directed to his court before the ambassador enters, are full of **resolute conviction** that either France will come under his control or he will destroy it. Advice to an actor should concentrate on **how** these lines must be delivered. Aspects of performance include **strength, tone and pace of the speaking voice**; and **posture, facial expression and movement**. Ask yourself **where** the King ought to be as these lines are spoken and **how** his delivery of the words should reinforce the emotion behind them.

   The second speech is much longer and a good answer will focus on **how the character and emotion develop** as the King becomes **more overtly threatening**. Is it appropriate for the actor to remain in the same position, or what movements would you recommend?

   You must explain **why** each direction to the actor is appropriate. **Quote** relevant lines from the play to support your view.

3. The last question often carries more marks and in recent exams candidates have been asked to write a short piece that continues the story in a different style. Here, your **ability to comprehend the dramatic situation** is being tested, along with the **skill of writing a short piece of dialogue**.

If the instructions are open-ended, any style of dialogue will be acceptable. Do not feel that you are expected to continue the Elizabethan register of Shakespeare. A **modern**, **colloquial** conversation between the ambassador and his master would be suitable, as long as you **capture the difficulty faced by the ambassador.** He must bring bad news to the Dauphin and diplomacy will prevent him from telling the bald truth.

The scene you write will be **short**, as you have very little time, but it could be **either serious or comical** in tone. The only real restriction is that it should include at least the **characters** of the ambassador and the Dauphin and it should be written in the form of **dialogue**.

> **key point**
>
> Always support your points with **evidence** from the text, dialogue or stage directions.

Conflict

All drama relies on **conflict** to generate and sustain the interest of the audience. Unseen passages usually involve conflict, such as the clash between King Henry and the French ambassador in the extract above.

Sometimes, however, the conflict is not simply between two opposing individuals or groups. It can occur **within the mind of a single person**. The following exam question illustrates this well, as there are a number of ways in which the **struggle between opposites** is dramatised here.

B   The following extract (in edited form) is taken from *Much Ado About Nothing* by William Shakespeare.
Read the extract and answer the questions that follow.

Background to the extract

Benedick and Beatrice are discussing Count Claudio and his bride-to-be, Hero. Mistakenly, Claudio thinks that Hero has been unfaithful to him and cancels their wedding. Beatrice weeps for her cousin Hero who, she strongly believes, has been wronged.

Much Ado About Nothing
William Shakespeare

Exeunt (all but Benedick and Beatrice)

BENEDICK:	(*With great kindness*) Lady Beatrice, have you wept all this while?
BEATRICE:	Yea, and I will weep a while longer.
BENEDICK:	I will not desire that.
BEATRICE:	You have no reason. I do it freely.
BENEDICK:	Surely I do believe your fair cousin is wronged.
BEATRICE:	Ah, how much might the man deserve of me that would right her!
BENEDICK:	Is there any way to show such friendship?
BEATRICE:	A very even way, but no such friend.
BENEDICK:	May a man do it?
BEATRICE:	It is a man's office, but not yours.
BENEDICK:	I do love nothing in the world so well as you. Is not that strange?
BEATRICE:	As strange as the thing I know not. It were as possible for me to say I loved nothing so well as you. But believe me not; and yet I lie not. I confess nothing, nor I deny nothing. I am sorry for my cousin.
BENEDICK:	By my sword, Beatrice, thou lovest me.
BEATRICE:	Do not swear, and eat it.

BENEDICK:	I will swear by it that you love me, and I will make him eat it that says I love not you.
BEATRICE:	Will you not eat your word?
BENEDICK:	With no sauce that can be devised to it. I protest I love thee.
BEATRICE:	Why then, God forgive me!
BENEDICK:	What offence, sweet Beatrice?
BEATRICE:	You have stayed me in a happy hour. I was about to protest I loved you.
BENEDICK:	And do it with all thy heart.
BEATRICE:	I love you with so much of my heart that none is left to protest.
BENEDICK:	Come, bid me do anything for thee.
BEATRICE:	(*Pause*) . . . Kill Claudio . . .
BENEDICK:	(*Horrified*) Ha! Not for the wide world!
BEATRICE:	(*Angrily*) You kill me to deny it. Farewell.
BENEDICK:	(*Calling out*) Wait, sweet Beatrice. (*Benedick tries to stop her leaving*)
BEATRICE:	I am gone, though I am here. There is no love in you. Nay, I pray you let me go.
BENEDICK:	Beatrice –
BEATRICE:	In faith, I will go.
BENEDICK:	We'll be friends first.
BEATRICE:	You dare easier be friends with me than fight with mine enemy.
BENEDICK:	Is Claudio thine enemy?
BEATRICE:	He is a villain, that hath slandered, scorned, dishonoured my kinswoman. O that I were a man! I would eat his heart in the market place.
BENEDICK:	(*Pleading*) Hear me, Beatrice!
BEATRICE:	Talk with a man out at a window! – a proper saying!
BENEDICK:	Nay but Beatrice –
BEATRICE:	Sweet Hero! She is wronged, she is slandered, she is undone.
BENEDICK:	Listen –
BEATRICE:	Princes and Counts! The goodly Count Claudio indeed! O that I had any friend would be a man for my sake! But manhood is melted into being courteous, giving compliments and having nice speech. There is no honour and truth anymore! I cannot be a man with wishing; therefore I will die a woman with grieving.
BENEDICK:	Wait, good Beatrice. By this hand, I love thee.
BEATRICE:	Use it for my love some other way than swearing by it.

BENEDICK:	Think you in your soul the Count Claudio hath wrong'd Hero?
BEATRICE:	Yea, as sure is I have a thought or a soul.
BENEDICK:	Enough, I am convinced. I will challenge him. I will kiss your hand, and so I leave you. By this hand, Claudio will meet his match. Think of me Beatrice. Go comfort your cousin: And so farewell.

(2005, Paper 2, Section (A), Shakespearean Drama)

Questions

Answer **two** of the following questions. Each question is worth 15 marks.

1. What is your impression of either Benedick or Beatrice from this extract? Support your answer by reference to the text.

2. Based on evidence from this extract, do you think Beatrice and Benedick are in love with each other? Support your answer by reference to the text.

3. Imagine this scene is to be staged and you are the director. Outline the directions you would give to either Beatrice or Benedick on how to perform their parts.

Explain your points clearly. Show **why** you hold certain beliefs about characters or how a scene should be produced.

Other drama

The **second option** for you in the **Unseen Drama** section is called **Other Drama**. This refers to any drama other than a Shakespeare play. In the past, there have been plays by a variety of authors of many different nationalities, ranging from ancient Greek drama to modern plays set in the present time.

Language

Since many of the plays in this section are set in **modern** times, the language will differ greatly from the style of English used by Shakespeare. Dialogue, if it attempts to be realistic, will imitate the speech of ordinary people. This **colloquial** style is evident in many modern plays.

Genre

The language used in a play helps us identify its genre. **Tragedies** will use language that establishes a serious atmosphere, while the lighter language of **comedies** suggests a happier outcome to events in the play. Some dramas will include a mixture of the serious and the trivial. This reflects our experience of the real world, where funny moments can happen in times of great trauma.

Character

As in Shakespearean plays, the language a character uses reveals a great deal about them. A character's **vocabulary** and **style of speaking** help the audience to form a view of their thoughts and feelings.

Costume, make-up and props

You should try to picture a scene as you read it. Imagine the colour and style of characters' **clothing**. Is it shabby or opulent? Make-up and props also help to convey character. **Props** may play a significant role in advancing the plot.

Voice, movement and posture

The way a character uses their **voice** tells us a lot. Do they speak gently or in an animated way? Colloquial language suggests that the actor will have to adopt a particular **accent**. The extract from *Amphibians* (on the next page) takes place in modern-day Wexford, so actors will have to adopt that particular accent.

   Movement and **posture** also communicate meaning. Does a character move around on stage or remain still? What kind of posture can they adopt to convey their inner feelings?

Lighting

Lighting helps to create atmosphere for a scene and modern drama is sometimes more demanding in this regard. Think about what is happening on stage and ask yourself what style of lighting would help the audience to relate to what they see.

Set

The set outlines the **world of the story** for us. A landscape tells us the play is set in the countryside, while skyscrapers in the background indicate that the story takes place in a modern city.

exam focus

You have **25** minutes to read and respond to the **Unseen Drama** question.

C   **The following extract is taken from *Amphibians* by Irish playwright Billy Roche. Read the extract and answer the questions that follow.**

Background to the extract

Amphibians is set in Wexford in the present day. Eagle is taking his son Isaac on a boat trip to Useless Island. He plans to spend the night on the uninhabited island as a way of teaching Isaac about growing up and taking responsibility in the adult world.

Amphibians
Billy Roche

ISAAC:	Look at all the stars, Da. Kind of electric stars. Not in the sky Da, in the water. What are they, anyway?
EAGLE:	Phosphorous.
ISAAC:	Phosphorous! I must tell them in school about that on Monday. I bet the teacher don't know about that.
EAGLE:	I'm feckin' sure he don't know about it.
ISAAC:	The size of that big eel boy! That fella'd nearly turn the boat over wouldn't he? Hah? What would ye do if he turned the boat over, Da?
EAGLE:	I don't know.
ISAAC:	Can you swim Da?
EAGLE:	Yeah of course I can swim.
ISAAC:	Can yeh? What's your favourite stroke?
EAGLE:	The Japanese flip-flop. Nothin' moves, only your tonsils.
ISAAC:	Yeah, 'help, help. . .' A full moon hah? Deadly looking ain't it?
EAGLE:	Yeah, yeh'd get up in the middle of the night to look at it sure.
ISAAC:	(*Chuckles*) That's a good one Da. You'd get up in the middle of the night to look at it. You'd hardly see it in the middle of the day would yeh? You should have been a comedian boy! (*Pause*)
EAGLE:	There she is Isaac. Useless Island. There seems to be a bit of an auld fog comin' down around her.
ISAAC:	Yeah, its queer spooky looking, ain't it?
EAGLE:	Not at all. (*Slight pause*)
ISAAC:	I don't think me Ma is exactly over the moon about all of this Da, is she?
EAGLE:	No, not exactly. Ah she's a bit nervous about it. Yeh see Isaac what she don't understand is that you and me are in our element out here like yeh know. What she don't seem to

realise is that this is our what-do-you-call-it . . . What's the word? Domain! But sure I suppose she's listenin' to the rest of them blackguardin' me all the time. I'm not coddin' yeh, for the past twelve months here you'd swear I was committing some sort of crime here just comin' out to work. I mean to say I'm only doin' what I always done. Yeh know? I come out here and I cast me nets and I sit and wait. What's wrong with that? Yeh know? No way am I in the wrong, I don't care what anyone says . . . Yeh know sometimes when I'm out here on me own in the middle of the night I'll stand up and I'll let a bit of an auld shout out of me. (*He shrieks*) I'm not coddin' yeh if anyone was watchin' me they'd have me feckin' certified so they would. But do yeh know why I do that? I do it to let this place know that I'm still here, that I'm still around. That's very important yeh know! That way the man learns to respect the place and the place'll respect the man. Me Da taught me that . . . Take a look back at the town.

ISAAC:	Oh yeah . . . All the lights! I wonder where our house is? I think I can see my pigeon loft Da. (*Eagle smiles at him tenderly*)
EAGLE:	As long as you do your best Isaac, that's all that matters yeh know. You must always do your best. And make the most of what yeh got . . .What's that? A seagull flyin' low be Jaysus!
ISAAC:	What do you mean?
EAGLE:	Search me. (*He chuckles and sits down again*) (*Pause*)
ISAAC:	Do yeh know somethin' Da, I don't think I ever saw you swimmin' . . . Da?
EAGLE:	What?
ISAAC:	I say I never saw you swimmin'.
EAGLE:	Why should I swim when I've got a boat? (*Pause. Lights down*)

Questions

1. What does the scene reveal about the character of Eagle? (10 marks)
2. The action in this scene takes place in a boat on a river at night. If you were the director of this play how would you create this illusion on a stage? (10 marks)
3. 'There is gentle humour in this scene but also a feeling of tension.' Discuss this view of the scene. (10 marks)

key point

Tension is an important element of drama. When you read a scene from any play, look out for any tension present. Consider **how** the playwright creates this tension.

The next extract also employs a very **colloquial** and **Irish** way of speaking. Again, there are images of water and boats, but here the mood is intensely sad.

 D **The following extract (in edited form) is taken from *Riders to the Sea* by Irish playwright J.M. Synge. Read the extract and answer the questions that follow.**

Background to the extract

Maurya, the principal character of the play, lives in a cottage on an island off the west coast of Ireland. She has had a long life of extreme hardship. Her husband and six of her sons, all fishermen, have been drowned at sea. In this scene, she and her daughters, Cathleen and Nora, learn of the drowning of the last of her sons, Michael and Bartley.

Riders to the Sea
J. M. Synge

CATHLEEN:	Michael is after being found in the far north.
MAURYA:	There does be a power of young men floating round in the sea, and what way would they know if it was Michael they had?
CATHLEEN:	It's Michael, God spare him, for they're after sending us a bit of his clothes from the far north.
	(*She reaches out and hands Maurya the clothes that belonged to Michael. Maurya stands up slowly, and takes them into her hands. Nora looks out.*)

NORA:	They're carrying a thing among them and there's water dripping out of it and leaving a track by the big stones.
CATHLEEN:	*(In a whisper to the women who have come in.)* Is it Bartley it is?
ONE OF THE WOMEN:	It is surely, God rest his soul. *(Two younger women come in and pull out the table. Then men carry in the body of Bartley, laid on a plank, with a bit of a sail over it, and lay it on the table.)*
CATHLEEN:	*(To the women, as they are doing so.)* What way was he drowned?
ONE OF THE WOMEN:	The gray pony knocked him into the sea, and he was washed out where there is a great surf on the white rocks.

(Maurya has gone over and knelt down at the head of the table. The women are keening [crying] softly and swaying themselves with a slow movement. Cathleen and Nora kneel at the other end of the table. The men kneel near the door.)

MAURYA:	*(Raising her head and speaking as if she did not see the people around her.)* They're all gone now, and there isn't anything more the sea can do to me . . . I'll have no call now to be up crying and praying when the wind breaks from the south, and you can hear the surf is in the east, and the surf is in the west, making a great stir with the two noises, and they hitting one on the other. I'll have no call now to be going down and getting Holy Water in the dark nights after Samhain, and I won't care what way the sea is when the other women will be keening. *(To Nora)* Give me the Holy Water, Nora, there's a small sup still on the dresser. *(Nora gives it to her. Maurya drops Michael's clothes across Bartley's feet, and sprinkles the Holy Water over him.)* It isn't that I haven't prayed for you, Bartley, to the Almighty God. It isn't that I haven't said prayers in the dark night till you wouldn't know what I'd be saying; but it's a great rest I'll have now, and it's time surely. It's a great rest I'll have now, and great sleeping in the long nights after Samhain, if it's only a bit of wet flour we do have to eat, and maybe a fish that would be stinking. *(She kneels down again, crossing herself, and saying prayers under her breath.)*

CATHLEEN:	(*To an old man kneeling near her.*) Maybe yourself and Eamon would make a coffin when the sun rises. We have fine white boards herself bought, God help her, thinking Michael would be found, and I have a new cake you can eat while you'll be working.
THE OLD MAN:	(*Looking at the boards.*) Are there nails with them?
CATHLEEN:	There are not, Colum; we didn't think of the nails.
ANOTHER MAN:	It's a great wonder she wouldn't think of the nails, and all the coffins she's seen made already.
CATHLEEN:	It's getting old she is, and broken. (*Maurya stands up again very slowly and spreads out the pieces of Michael's clothes beside the body, sprinkling them with the last of the Holy Water.*)
NORA:	(*In a whisper to Cathleen.*) She's quiet now and easy; but the day Michael was drowned you could hear her crying out from this to the spring well. It's fonder she was of Michael, and would any one have thought that?
CATHLEEN:	(*Slowly and clearly.*) An old woman will be soon tired with anything she will do, and isn't it nine days herself is after crying and keening, and making great sorrow in the house?
MAURYA:	(*Puts the empty cup mouth downwards on the table, and lays her hands together on Bartley's feet.*) They're all together this time, and the end is come. May the Almighty God have mercy on Bartley's soul, and on Michael's soul, and on the souls of Sheamus and Patch, and Stephen and Shawn (*Bending her head*); and may He have mercy on my soul, Nora, and on the soul of every one is left living in the world. (*She pauses, and the keen rises a little more loudly from the women, then sinks away. Continuing.*) Michael has a clean burial in the far north, by the grace of the Almighty God. Bartley will have a fine coffin out of the white boards, and a deep grave surely. What more can we want than that? No man at all can be living for ever, and we must be satisfied. (*She kneels down again and the curtain falls slowly.*)

(2000, Paper 2, Section 1(B), Other Drama)

Questions

Answer **two** of the following questions. **Each question is worth 15 marks**.

1. What type of character do you imagine Maurya to be? Support your answer by reference to the text.
2. How is the language of the extract different from the language that we use today? Select features of the language to illustrate the differences.
3. Imagine you are the producer of this scene. It is most important to create an appropriate atmosphere and setting. Give a description of the set (props, stage layout), costumes, lighting and any other aid you would use to create this atmosphere and setting.

Studied drama

The **second** question you **must** answer in the Drama section is a question on a play you studied in class. If you have seen a performance of the play (either on stage or a film version) you should make use of this in your answer. Knowledge of stagecraft and precise reference to specific productions of your studied drama will merit higher marks in the exam.

Below are some recurring questions on the studied drama:

- Discussion of a **central character** in the play.
- **Themes** or issues explored by the play.
- **Key scenes** or moments of great importance.
- **Directing a scene** from the play.
- **Relationships** between characters, including conflict.
- Dramatic **development of the story**, leading to a climax.
- **Personal response** to characters, scenes or themes.
- The **world of the play** expressed through attitudes and values.

key point

When revising studied drama, **make clear notes** of all the important details in the play.

This is not an exhaustive list. Certain new approaches may emerge, but the key factors of good drama remain the same. If you **prepare answers** for a reasonable **range** of these questions, you will have enough material to answer this question very well in the exam.

In order to revise efficiently, you need to **identify the following**:

- Your **favourite character** and **why** you like that person so much.
- Your **favourite moment** in the play and the **reason** it held your attention so well.
- The **opening** scene.
- The moment of greatest **dramatic tension** in the play (the **climax**).
- How the **key problem** or question was **resolved** or concluded.

If you select and learn these aspects well, you will have more than enough material to deal with this section of the drama.

For each scene you revise you must know:

- **What** happens.
- **Who** is involved.
- **Key quotations** from the text.

Avoid writing a mere summary of the action of the play. Instead, your answer should focus on discussing the question by making **precise points**, backing them up with **quotations** and **explaining** what you mean.

The exam question below demands that you give **clear information**, **show** that you know the **text** and **explain** your **own response** to the **action** of the scene.

1. Name a play you have studied.
2. Choose a scene from this play you found either happy **or** sad. Describe how the playwright conveys this happiness or sadness.   (30 marks)

(2004, Paper 1, Section 1, Drama)

SAMPLE ANSWER

My favourite scene from *Romeo and Juliet* by William Shakespeare is **Act 2, Scene 2**. This scene takes place in Juliet Capulet's garden at night time, after the feast where the 'star-crossed lovers' meet for the very first time. I enjoyed this scene above all others because it is the **happiest scene** in the play. In my opinion, the hero and heroine are never quite as happy at any other point in the story.

It begins in a **comical** way, as Juliet is high on a balcony while Romeo is beneath her in the garden hidden from her view. Romeo is **happy because** he has fallen in love, again! Seeing his new love appear lit up in the window, he joyfully declares that 'Juliet is the sun'.

This happy **metaphor** is just the first of many beautiful **images** in this scene. I really like Romeo's lines when he sees Juliet leaning out, resting her cheek on her hand:

'O that I were a glove upon that hand,
That I might touch that cheek!'

This is a very intimate and pleasant wish and we enjoy hearing Romeo express it because we know his wish will be granted when he embraces Juliet later.

It is a happy scene because Juliet's wishes also come true. Unaware of the fact that she is being spied on by Romeo, she wistfully regrets that a mere name divides them from each other. Referring to Romeo as a beautiful flower, she insists that 'that which we call a rose by any other word would smell as sweet'. The fact that she is unhappy thinking they will never be lovers adds to the eventual happiness of the scene, since we know Romeo is about to appear and declare his love.

All the **barriers** between them, as members of the feuding Montague and Capulet clans, are **overcome** when Romeo bravely scales the wall and climbs up to kiss her. In this scene, the ridiculous **proposal of marriage** is a happy **antidote** to the vicious antagonism of the '**ancient grudge**' the families bear for one another. When Romeo begs her ('Wilt thou leave me so unsatisfied'), the audience shares in his joy that she accepts him and the impossible dream comes true as they are engaged, in spite of all the obstacles to their love.

Shakespeare realistically mixes happiness with sadness at the end of this scene because the lovers must say goodbye. Juliet expresses this perfectly when she tells him that 'parting is such sweet sorrow'. Even though Romeo must leave, we are happy in the knowledge that Juliet will be reunited with him soon.

COMMENT

- The candidate clearly **identifies** a **happy scene** from the play.
- A good **explanation for Romeo's happiness** is given, well **supported** by both **reference and quotation**.
- Juliet's feelings are also explored and, crucially, the **personal response** of the candidate to this scene is **outlined and analysed.**

Sample exam paper

Answer **QUESTION ONE** and **QUESTION TWO**

QUESTION ONE (30)

Answer **either (A) or (B).**

(A) SHAKESPEAREAN DRAMA

The following extract (in edited form) is taken from *Antony and Cleopatra* by William Shakespeare. Read the extract carefully and then answer the questions which follow.

Background to this extract
Cleopatra is an Egyptian queen who falls in love with Antony, a Roman officer and nobleman. Antony is recalled to Rome and while there marries Caesar's sister, Octavia, for political reasons. Before this extract, Cleopatra remembers Antony fondly and eagerly awaits his return to Egypt.

In this extract a messenger arrives with news from Rome and Cleopatra's mood changes. She questions the messenger and learns about Antony's marriage. Her advisor, Charmian, is also present.

CLEOPATRA:	[*warmly*] Prithee, friend [the messenger],
	Tell me the news from Rome,
	The good and bad together. He's [Antony] friends with
	Caesar; In good health, thou sayst; and thou sayst, unmarried.
MESSENGER:	Unmarried, madam! no; I made no such report:
	Madam, he's married to Octavia.
CLEOPATRA:	I am pale!
CLEOPATRA:	The most infectious disease upon thee! [*Strikes him down.*]
MESSENGER:	Good madam, patience.
CLEOPATRA:	What say you? Hence, [*Strikes him again.*]
	Horrible villain! I'll unhair thy head: [*She pulls at him.*]
	Thou shalt be whipp'd with wire, and stew'd in brine*, *salt*
	Smarting* in vinegar. *feeling pain*
MESSENGER:	Gracious madam.
CLEOPATRA:	Say 'tis not so, I will give thee land,
	And make thy fortunes proud,
	And I will give thee a gift beside as well.
MESSENGER:	He's married, madam.
CLEOPATRA:	Rogue! thou hast liv'd too long. [*Draws a knife.*]
MESSENGER:	Nay, then I'll run.
	What mean you, madam? I have done no wrong. [*Exit.*]
CHARMIAN:	Good madam, keep yourself within yourself;
	The man is innocent.
CLEOPATRA:	Some innocents 'scape not the thunderbolt.
	Call the slave again: Though I am mad, I will not bite him.
	Call.
CHAMAIN:	He is afeard to come.
CLEOPATRA:	I will not hurt him.
	These hands do lack nobility, that they strike out in a mean
	way.

Re-enter Charmian, and Messenger.

CLEOPATRA:	Come hither, sir.
	Though it be honest, it is never good to bring bad news.
	Tell me now the truth, is he married?

MESSENGER:	He's married, madam.
CLEOPATRA:	The gods confound thee! Holds' thou still to that tale?
MESSENGER:	Should I lie, madam?
CLEOPATRA:	O! I would thou didst,
	Go, get thee hence.
MESSENGER:	I crave your highness' pardon.
CLEOPATRA:	He is married?
MESSENGER:	To punish me for what you make me tell
	Seems most unfair; he's married to Octavia.
CLEOPATRA:	Get thee hence.

[*Exit* Messenger.]

CHARMIAN:	Good your highness, patience.
CLEOPATRA:	Lead me from hence; I faint. O Charmian!
	Go to the messenger, bid him
	Report the feature* of Octavia: her years, *appearance*
	Let him not leave out the colour of her hair,
	Her height, her temperament.
	Bring me word quickly.
	Pity me, Charmian,
	But do not speak to me. Lead me to my chamber. [*Exeunt.*]

Answer **two** of the following questions. Each question is worth 15 marks.

1. What is your impression of Cleopatra from this extract? Support your answer with reference to the text.

2. Imagine you are the messenger in this extract. Write a short dialogue between yourself and your friend about your experience with the Queen. Tell your friend what happened and explain how you feel after your encounter with Cleopatra. Base your answer on information from the text.

3. Imagine that you are directing this play. In the context of the extract you have just read explain how you would make use of **TWO** of the following in your production: costume, setting, facial expression, props.

(B) OTHER DRAMA

The following extract (in edited form) is adapted from a play by Simon Reade based on Michael Morpurgo's novel *Private Peaceful*. Read the extract carefully and answer the questions which follow.

Background to this extract

In this extract two brothers, Tommo and Charlie Peaceful, are part of an English regiment fighting in the trenches of World War I. Although both brothers have been injured their Commanding Officer, Sergeant Hanley, expects them to fight on with the rest of the troops.

Ypres, France, 24th June 1916. No-man's-land.

CHARLIE:	Thought we'd lost you, Tommo. The same shell that buried you killed half a dozen of the others. You were lucky. Your head looks a bit of a mess, though. Me, I can't feel my legs. I think I've lost a lot of blood.
TOMMO:	Where are we, Charlie?
CHARLIE:	Middle of bloody no-man's-land, that's where, some old German dug-out.
TOMMO:	We'd best stay here for a while, hadn't we, Charlie?
SERGEANT HANLEY:	Stay put? Stay put? You're worse than your brother, Peaceful. Our orders are to press home the attack and then hold our ground. Only fifty yards or so to the German trenches. On your feet, all of you. *(No one moves.)*
SERGEANT HANLEY:	What in hell's name is the matter with you lot? On your feet, damn you! On your feet!
TOMMO:	I think we are all thinking the same thing, Sergeant. You take us out there now and the machine guns will mow us down. Maybe we should stay here and then go back later when it gets dark? No point in going out there and getting ourselves killed for nothing, is there Sergeant?
SERGEANT HANLEY:	Are you disobeying my order, Private Peaceful?
TOMMO:	No, I'm just letting you know what I think. What we all think.

SERGEANT HANLEY:	And I'm telling you, Peaceful, that if you don't come with us when we go, it'll be a court martial for you. It'll be the firing squad. Do you hear me, Peaceful? Do you hear me?
TOMMO:	Yes, Sergeant. I hear you. But the thing is Sergeant, even if I wanted to, I can't go with you because I'd have to leave Charlie behind, and I can't do that. He's wounded. I don't think he can walk, let alone run. I'm not leaving him.
SERGEANT HANLEY:	You miserable little worm, Peaceful. I should shoot you right where you are and save the firing squad the trouble. The rest of you, on your feet. I want you men out there. It's a court martial for anyone who stays. (*Screaming*) Let's go! Let's go! (*Sound : the German machine guns open fire.*)
CHARLIE:	I'm not sure I'll make it, Tommo. I want you to have this. (*Charlie takes off his watch*) It's a wonderful watch. It will never let you down. If you wind it regular, time will never stop and when you get back home, my little Tommo can have it. He's got all the time in the world.

Answer **two** of the following questions. Each question is worth 15 marks.

1. What is your impression of Tommo from this extract? Support your answer with reference to the text.

2. Write a short dialogue between Sergeant Hanley and Tommo that follows on from the end of this extract. Keep your dialogue true to what you know of Sergeant Hanley and Tommo's characters from this extract.

3. Imagine you are directing this play. In the context of the extract you have just read, explain how you would make use of **TWO** of the following in your production: setting, sound effects, props, costumes.

QUESTION ONE   (30)

Answer **EITHER 1 OR 2** which follow.

N.B. You must give the name of the play that you choose. You may **NOT** choose either of the scenes quoted on this examination paper as the basis for your answer.

1. Choose a scene from a play you have studied where a particular mood or atmosphere is created.

   (i) Describe the mood or atmosphere in this scene. Support your answer with reference to the text. (15 marks)

   (ii) How does the playwright create this mood or atmosphere? Aspects you may wish to consider could include: setting, lighting, stage directions, music, sound or dialogue. (15 marks)

   OR

2. From a play you have studied choose **one** important relationship.

   (i) Describe the main characteristics of this relationship throughout the play. (15 marks)

   (ii) How does **either** the setting (time or place) **or** another character have an influence on this relationship? Support your answer with reference to the text. (15 marks)

   (2009, Paper 2, Section 1, Drama)

6 Poetry

Read	Revised	Recapped

 aims

- To **respond** to poems.
- To identify a **variety of themes**.
- To learn **critical analysis** of poetry.
- To explain **poetic technique**.

You will answer two poetry questions in your Junior Certificate exam: **Unseen Poetry** and **Studied Poetry**. There is usually a connecting theme or idea between these questions. Developing the skill of **personal response** to poetry is essential and in order to ensure this, you must practise a **range** of Unseen Poetry questions.

Unseen poetry

Ten unseen poems are presented below. Each poem has accompanying exercises, which are based on typical exam questions. Spend **25 minutes** on each question.

Steps for responding to unseen poems
- **Read the poem** carefully and **highlight five key words** or phrases.
- Underline any **images** that stand out for you.
- Note any **sound effects** in the **language**.
- Now **read the question** and consult the notes you have made.
- **Trust** your **instincts** and **explain** your response by **commenting on quotes** from the poem.

A **key word** or phrase is any word or group of words that makes an immediate impression on you. It could be because it evokes a strong feeling or provokes you to think in a new way about a topic. A key word could be one that puzzles you or is amusing for some reason.

   Images in poetry are pictures in your head created by the words the poet uses to describe something.

   Sound effects include:
- **Rhyme:** when words sound alike, usually at the ends of lines of poetry.
- **Rhythm:** a regular pattern of beats or syllables in a line of poetry.
- **Alliteration:** the repetition of consonants, especially at the beginnings of words close to each other.

- **Assonance:** the repetition of identical vowel sounds in words that appear close together.
- **Cacophony:** repetition of harsh sounds.
- **Euphony:** repetition of pleasant or sweet sounds.
- **Onomatopoeia:** when the sound of a word echoes its meaning, e.g. fizz, plop, moo.

You may notice some of these features as you read a poem. Ask yourself **why** the poet chose the sound effect. Does it **echo** or match something being said in the poem?

 A **The poem 'Born Yesterday' was written by Philip Larkin to celebrate the birth of his best friend's daughter, Sally. Read the poem carefully and answer all three questions that follow. You should support the points you make with quotations from the poem.**

Born Yesterday
for Sally Amis

Philip Larkin

Tightly-folded bud,
I have wished you something
None of the others would:
Not the usual stuff
About being beautiful,
Or running off a spring
Of innocence and love –
They will all wish you that,
And should it prove possible,
Well, you're a lucky girl.

But if it shouldn't, then
May you be ordinary;
Have, like other women,
An average of talents:
Not ugly, not good-looking,
Nothing uncustomary
To pull you off balance,
That, unworkable itself,
Stops all the rest from working.
In fact, may you be dull –
If that is what a skilled,
Vigilant, flexible,
Unemphasised, enthralled
Catching of happiness is called.

1. What are the poet's wishes for the girl as she grows up? (10 marks)
2. If you were one of the baby's parents would you be pleased with this poem? Explain your answer. (10 marks)
3. Do you think that this is a well-written poem? Explain your point of view with reference to the text of the poem. (10 marks)

Hints for approaching these questions

1. The first question about the poem 'Born Yesterday' asks about the poet's wishes for the new baby girl. This implies that he has **several** wishes or hopes for the child as she gets older. In the first stanza he uses the **verb 'wish'** twice. **Look closely** at what he is saying here.

   You may also notice that the poet **contrasts** his own hopes for Sally with the wishes of 'all the others'. Clearly he feels that his vision of her future is unusual in some way. A further **clue** in the second stanza is when he says 'May you be . . . .' Here he is telling us what he hopes will happen as she matures.

   The remainder of the poem is a development or explanation of this wish as he clarifies what he means in a **list of certain qualities**. These adjectives really give the strongest idea of the kind of person the poet hopes Sally will become.

2. The second question requires you to show that you know the poet's hopes for the child. Once you identify again the essential detail of his ambition for her, you are free to argue either that you would be **happy or unhappy** with the poet's wish. The essential thing is to **explain why** you would be pleased or displeased and **refer to words or phrases** from the poem in writing your answer.

3. The final question relating to 'Born Yesterday' is typical of recent exam questions and does require you to have a clear idea of **what it is that makes a poem work.**

A really good poem will evoke a **strong feeling** in the reader. How do you **react** on first reading the poem? If you do have a clear response, then you may argue that the poem is well-written because it has a definite **emotional effect** on you. Show **how** this happens by **quoting** the precise words and **explaining** your reaction to them.

Imagery or **sound effects** can also contribute to the overall impact a poem makes. You might say that the poem is good because a particular image is compelling, or because of the effect of rhyme or alliteration.

Another option is to say **how** the poem **makes you think about life** in a new or interesting way. The best poetry challenges our beliefs about ourselves and the world around us.

exam Q

B   **Read the poem 'In Memory of George Best' by Dermot Bolger and answer both of the questions that follow.**

In Memory of George Best
Dermot Bolger

In one corner of our minds it remains 1969:
Frosted pavements, icy breath, yet our hands thaw

In the thrill of chasing a ball under streetlights,
Voices in the dark calling the names of Best and Law.

A drudge of decades have clogged our arteries,
Yet no matter what occurred, what we have become,

When we see again his feint, his sheer artistry
Thousands of us are instantaneously made young.

Questions
1. What images does the poet recall from his childhood?   (15 marks)
2. How would you describe the tone of the poem?   (15 marks)

SAMPLE ANSWERS

ANSWER 1

The poet remembers **playing football with his friends** in the streets in 1969. The death of George Best reminds him of 'the thrill of chasing a ball under streetlights'. As a child he was inspired to play by the 'sheer artistry' of his heroes.

Another image is of the **cold weather as the boys played**, in spite of the 'frosted pavements and icy breath' of wintertime.

Bolger also creates for us the **sounds he heard as he played football.** He and his pals called out to each other 'the names of Best and Law', pretending to be famous soccer players.

COMMENT
- **Three relevant points** are made about images in the poem. Each point is **developed** in a short paragraph.
- The student **illustrates** his points well by including **four relevant quotations**.

ANSWER 2

The tone or feeling of this poem is **nostalgic**. The death of his hero, George Best, makes the poet **remember the good times** when he was young. When he thinks again about 'chasing a ball under streetlights' he feels happy.

The poet also feels **regret** that he is no longer a child enjoying the fun of a street game. Since 1969, a 'drudge of decades' has passed and his life is not as exciting as it used to be.

I think he feels **surprised** that his hero's 'sheer artistry' can work like magic on so many people who are 'instantaneously made young'. Bolger is sad that George Best is dead, but **grateful** that this footballer brought him so much pleasure in his life.

COMMENT
- The first sentence **identifies** a **tone of nostalgia**.
- **Feelings** of happiness, regret, excitement, surprise, sadness and gratitude are also referred to in this **comprehensive description** of the tone of the poem.

C **Read the poem 'Fireworks' by James Reeves and answer the questions that follow. Your answer should refer to words or phrases in the poem in order to support the points you make.**

Fireworks

James Reeves

They rise like sudden fiery flowers
That burst upon the night,
Then fall to earth in burning showers
Of crimson, blue and white.

Like buds too wonderful to name,
Each miracle unfolds
And Catherine wheels begin to flame
Like whirling marigolds.

Rockets and Roman candles make
An orchard of the sky,
Where magic trees their petals shake
Upon each gazing eye.

Questions

1. Choose any interesting **metaphor** in the poem and say why you like it.

   (10 marks)
2. How does the writer **evoke sound** in the poem?   (10 marks)
3. Describe the **atmosphere** or mood created in this poem.   (10 marks)

D   **Read 'Miracle on St David's Day' by Gillian Clarke and answer two of the questions that follow.**

Miracle on St David's Day

Gillian Clarke

'They flash upon that inward eye
Which is the bliss of solitude'
'The Daffodils' by William Wordsworth.

An afternoon yellow and open-mouthed
with daffodils. The sun treads the path
among cedars and enormous oaks.
It might be a country house, guests strolling,
the rumps of gardeners between nursery shrubs.

I am reading poetry to the insane.
An old woman, interrupting, offers
as many buckets of coal as I need.
A beautiful chestnut-haired boy listens
entirely absorbed. A schizophrenic

on a good day, they tell me later.
In a cage of first March sun, a woman
sits not listening, not seeing, not feeling.
In her neat clothes the woman is absent.
A big, mild man is tenderly led

to his chair. He has never spoken.
His labourer's hands on his knees, he rocks
gently to the rhythms of the poems.
I read to their presences, absences,
to the big, dumb labouring man as he rocks.

He is suddenly standing, silently,
huge and mild, but I feel afraid. Like slow
movement of spring water or the first bird
of the year in the breaking darkness,
the labourer's voice recites, 'The Daffodils'.

The nurses are frozen, alert; the patients
seem to listen. He is hoarse but word-perfect.
Outside the daffodils are still as wax,
a thousand, ten thousand, their syllables
unspoken, their creams and yellows still.

Forty years ago, in a Valleys school,
the class recited poetry by rote.
Since the dumbness of misery fell
he has remembered there was a music
of speech and that once he had something to say.

When he's done, before the applause, we observe
the flowers' silence. A thrush sings
and the daffodils are flame.

key point

Any poem you read here
may be learned and used
in the **Studied Poetry**
section of the exam.

Questions

1. What is the miracle to which the title refers? (10 marks)
2. The poet reads for an unusual audience. Describe her audience in this poem. (10 marks)
3. What does the poet reveal about the power of our imagination? (10 marks)

E **Read 'Carentan O Carentan' by Louis Simpson and answer the questions that follow.**

Carentan O Carentan

Louis Simpson

Trees in the old days used to stand
And shape a shady lane
Where lovers wandered hand in hand
Who came from Carentan.

This was the shining green canal
Where we came two by two
Walking at combat-interval.
Such trees we never knew.

The day was early June, the ground
Was soft and bright with dew.
Far away the guns did sound,
But here the sky was blue.

The sky was blue, but there a smoke
Hung still above the sea
Where the ships together spoke
To towns we could not see.

Could you have seen us through a glass
You would have said a walk
Of farmers out to turn the grass.
Each with his own hay-fork.

The watchers in their leopard suits
Waited till it was time,
And aimed between the belt and boot
And let the barrel climb.

I must lie down at once, there is
A hammer at my knee.
And call it death or cowardice,
Don't count again on me.

Everything's all right, Mother,
Everyone gets the same
At one time or another.
It's all in the game.

I never strolled, nor ever shall,
Down such a leafy lane.
I never drank in a canal,
Nor ever shall again.

There is a whistling in the leaves
And it is not the wind,
The twigs are falling from the knives
That cut men to the ground.

Tell me, Master-Sergeant,
The way to turn and shoot.
But the Sergeant's silent
That taught me how to do it.

Captain, show us quickly
Our place upon the map.
But the Captain's sickly
And taking a long nap.

Lieutenant, what's my duty,
My place in the platoon?
He too's a sleeping beauty,
Charmed by that strange tune.

Carentan O Carentan
Before we met with you
We never yet had lost a man
Or knew what death could do.

Questions

1. There are many contrasting images in the poem. What is the effect of these contrasts? (10 marks)
2. How does the speaker feel about the town of Carentan? (10 marks)
3. Suggest an alternative title for this poem and explain your title with detailed reference to the text of the poem. (10 marks)

 F   **Read 'Watching Walls' by Mary O'Gorman and answer the questions that follow.**

Watching Walls

Mary O'Gorman

Pull yourself together; he implores
I watch walls edge across black floors.

Don't turn back now daughters protest
Their incline is my Everest.

Pick up that phone, my close friends coax
As they make tea, make sense, make jokes.

Let's try new pills, the doctor sighs,
I stare at the spiders in his eyes.

Please try to sleep, a ward nurse begs,
There's a cobwebbed Christ on the window ledge.

How did this happen, my dead mother asks
Tormented butterflies batter the glass.

Questions

1. How does the poet convey the pain of depression in this poem? (10 marks)
2. Which image do you find most effective? Explain your choice. (10 marks)
3. What feelings does the poem create in you? (10 marks)

Always **explain your points,** referring to the **key words or phrases** in the poem.

G **Read 'Coming' by Philip Larkin and answer the questions that follow.**

Coming

Philip Larkin

On longer evenings,
Light, chill and yellow,
Bathes the serene
Foreheads of houses.
A thrush sings,
Laurel-surrounded
In the deep bare garden,
Its fresh-peeled voice
Astonishing the brickwork.

It will be spring soon,
It will be spring soon –
And I, whose childhood
Is a forgotten boredom,
Feel like a child
Who comes on a scene
Of adult reconciling,
And can understand nothing
But the unusual laughter,
And starts to be happy.

Questions

1. What alerts the poet to the approach of spring?　　　　　　(10 marks)
2. How does he explain his feelings about the arrival of the new season?
　　　　　　　　　　　　　　　　　　　　　　　　　　　(10 marks)
3. Would you like to read more of Philip Larkin's poetry? Based on the evidence from this poem give reasons for your answer.　　　(10 marks)

Unseen Poetry questions often require you to express your **personal opinion**. Remember to **back up your ideas** with **quotation** from the poem and **explanations**.

exam Q H **Read 'The Charge of the Light Brigade' by Alfred, Lord Tennyson and answer two of the questions that follow.**

The Charge of the Light Brigade

Alfred, Lord Tennyson

Half a league, half a league,
Half a league onward,
All in the valley of Death
Rode the six hundred.
'Forward, the Light Brigade!
Charge for the guns!' he said:
Into the valley of Death
Rode the six hundred.

'Forward, the Light Brigade!'
Was there a man dismayed?
Not though the soldier knew
Someone had blundered:
Their's not to make reply,
Their's not to reason why,
Their's but to do and die:
Into the valley of Death
Rode the six hundred.

Cannon to right of them,
Cannon to left of them,
Cannon in front of them
Volleyed and thundered;
Stormed at with shot and shell,
Boldly they rode and well,
Into the jaws of Death,
Into the mouth of Hell
Rode the six hundred.

Flashed all their sabres bare,
Flashed as they turned in air
Sabring the gunners there,
Charging an army, while
All the world wondered:

Plunged in the battery-smoke
Right through the line they broke;
Cossack and Russian
Reeled from the sabre-stroke
Shattered and sundered.
Then they rode back, but not
Not the six hundred.

Cannon to right of them,
Cannon to left of them,
Cannon behind them
Volleyed and thundered;
Stormed at with shot and shell,
While horse and hero fell,
They that had fought so well
Came through the jaws of Death,
Back from the mouth of Hell,
All that was left of them,
Left of six hundred.

When can their glory fade?
O the wild charge they made!
All the world wondered.
Honor the charge they made!
Honor the Light Brigade,
Noble six hundred!

Questions

1. What is the attitude of the soldiers as they charge? (10 marks)
2. Comment on the poet's use of rhythm, rhyme and repetition. (10 marks)
3. Choose an image from the poem that you found striking and say why it is effective. (10 marks)

 I Read 'Leaning into the afternoons . . . ' by Pablo Neruda and answer the questions that follow.

Leaning into the afternoons . . .

Pablo Neruda

Leaning into the afternoons I cast my sad nets
towards your oceanic eyes.

There in the highest blaze my solitude lengthens and flames,
its arms turning like a drowning man's.

I send out red signals across your absent eyes
that wave like the sea or the beach by a lighthouse.

You keep only darkness, my distant female,
from your regard sometimes the coast of dread emerges.

Leaning into the afternoons I fling my sad nets
to that sea that is thrashed by your oceanic eyes.

The birds of night peck at the first stars
that flash like my soul when I love you.

The night gallops on its shadowy mare
shedding blue tassels over the land.

Questions

1. The speaker in this love poem is a fisherman. How does he make use of his knowledge of the sea in expressing his love? (15 marks)
2. Describe the woman he addresses in this poem. (15 marks)
3. Do you think this is a good love poem? Give reasons for your answer based on evidence from the poem. (15 marks)

exam Q   J   **Read 'Pike' by Ted Hughes and answer the questions that follow.**

Pike

Pike, three inches long, perfect
Pike in all parts, green tigering the gold.
Killers from the egg: the malevolent aged grin.
They dance on the surface among the flies.

Or move, stunned by their own grandeur,
Over a bed of emerald, silhouette
Of submarine delicacy and horror.
A hundred feet long in their world.

In ponds, under the heat-struck lily pads —
Gloom of their stillness:
Logged on last year's black leaves, watching upwards.
Or hung in an amber cavern of weeds

The jaws' hooked clamp and fangs
Not to be changed at this date:
A life subdued to its instrument,
The gills kneading quietly, and the pectorals.

Three we kept behind glass,
Jungled in weed: three inches, four,
And four and a half: fed fry to them —
Suddenly there were two. Finally one

With a sag belly and the grin it was born with.
And indeed they spare nobody.
Two, six pounds each, over two feet long,
High and dry and dead in the willow-herb —

One jammed past its gills down the other's gullet:
The outside eye stared: as a vice locks —
The same iron in this eye
Though its film shrank in death.

A pond I fished, fifty yards across,
Whose lilies and muscular tench
Had outlasted every visible stone
Of the monastery that planted them —

Stilled legendary depth:
It was as deep as England. It held
Pike too immense to stir, so immense and old
That past nightfall I dared not cast

But silently cast and fished
With the hair frozen on my head
For what might move, for what eye might move.
The still splashes on the dark pond,

Owls hushing the floating woods
Frail on my ear against the dream
Darkness beneath night's darkness had freed,
That rose slowly towards me, watching.

Questions

1. Nature is one of the themes of 'Pike'. What does the poem tell us about the natural world? Explain your answer with reference to the poem.   (15 marks)

2. How would you describe the mood or atmosphere created by Ted Hughes in this poem? Illustrate your answer with reference to the words of the poem.
(15 marks)

key point

Always read a poem carefully and pay attention to the **thoughts and feelings** it **evokes** for you.

Studied poetry

In the course of your three years as a Junior Certificate student you have read many poems. The **Studied Poetry** question tests **your understanding** of the poems you have explored in class. You must **select a group** of up to **ten** poems in order to be able to answer the **range** of possible questions in this section. Your choice of poems should be based on your answers to the following questions:

1. Name the **poem you like the best** and the **poem you like the least. Explain,** by **comparing** the two, **why** you like one and dislike the other.
2. Name **two poems** (written by **different poets**) that deal with a **similar theme.**
3. Identify **a poet whose work you enjoy** and give the titles of **two** of their poems that you have studied.
4. Select **two poems** you have studied that contain **curious or interesting images.**
5. Find **two poems** where the poet has made clever use of the **sounds of words.**
6. Choose **two poems** that arouse **intense feelings in you.**

In choosing poems, you will find that some poems will satisfy more than one of the criteria above. For example, two of the poems in this chapter have the **theme of war**: 'Carentan O Carentan' and 'The Charge of the Light Brigade'. Both poems also contain **interesting images** and the Tennyson poem in particular makes clever use of the **sounds of words.** You might also include the **two poems by the poet Philip Larkin.** Which of the Larkin poems was your favourite? 'Coming' deals with the themes of nature and childhood and has several examples of **powerful metaphors.**

In order to be fully prepared for your Studied Poetry question, you should know the **title** of the poem, the **name of the poet** and a **number of useful quotations.** The Poetry question requires you to examine the poem carefully and give a focused answer. It is vital to support your answer with **precise and accurate quotations** from the poem. Some of your poems will be short and easier to learn because of the poet's use of **rhyme, rhythm** and other sound effects.

Above all, you must give some thought to the **reasons** for choosing certain poems. Many questions require you to give your own **personal response** to a favourite poem or to show how a poem helped you to make sense of some area of your own life. For this reason, you must be able to say **why** you have chosen certain poems.

It is also important to know the meaning of some of the **technical words** used in discussing poetry. The **glossary of figures of speech** on p. 33 will be useful for you in this regard. Familiarise yourself with this glossary.

Answer **EITHER 1 OR 2** which follow.

1. From the poetry studied by you choose a poem which is set in an interesting time **or** place.
   (a) Describe the setting.
   (b) What does this setting contribute to the effectiveness of the poem? Give reasons for your answer based on evidence from the poem. (30 marks)

OR

2. From the poetry you have studied choose a poem which deals with either youth **or** old age.
   (a) What pictures does this poem give of either youth **or** old age?
   (b) What is your personal response to the picture of youth **or** old age given in the poem? Support your answer with reference to the poem. (30 marks)

(2005, Paper 2, Section 2, Poetry)

SAMPLE ANSWERS

ANSWER 1(a)

A poem I studied called '**Carentan O Carentan**' is set in an interesting time and place. The **location** is also the name of the poem: Carentan is a town or village described by the poet in great detail. Louis Simpson tells us about the 'shady lane where lovers wandered' and of the 'shining green canal' that flows through the town. This pleasant scene takes place in 'early June', probably in the morning as the 'ground was soft and bright with dew'. The trees, the canal, and the soft, bright dew give us an impression of a **tranquil pastoral setting**.

We discover, however, that there is something **sinister** about this location at this precise moment. The speaker and his friends are being observed by 'watchers in their leopard suits' and this **illusion of peace** is about to be torn apart. Carentan is now the location for an ambush. In **contrast** to the earlier picture of **calm beauty** is the scene of **carnage**, the 'whistling in the leaves' is 'not the wind' but a hail of gunfire. The setting therefore is both **beautiful and horrific**. Carentan is remembered not only for its picturesque charm but also as a war zone and the scene of a massacre.

COMMENT

- This answer **explains** that 'Carentan O Carentan' takes place in a **beautiful setting** that becomes even more 'interesting' because it is the scene of a **dramatic attack**.
- A **detailed description** is given by means of well-chosen **quotations**.
- The **two paragraphs** of the answer offer **analysis** of the **contrasting depictions** of the setting.

ANSWER 1(b)

The initial setting of tranquil beauty creates a **relaxed mood** in the poem 'Carentan O Carentan'. 'The sky was blue' and the poet tells us the men looked like a group of 'farmers out to turn the grass'. In a scene like this we expect something pleasant to happen. The poet even refers to Carentan as a place where 'lovers wandered hand in hand'. **Instead of love or beauty the scene becomes one of horror and violence.**

The **contrast** between the two scenes makes the poem very **dramatic**. We are surprised by the ferocious attack 'that cut men to the ground'. Instead of a relaxing stroll, the journey is a fatal walk into the jaws of a trap. I think this is very effective because the **stark change emphasises how awful the ambush must have been**. Also, just like the soldiers, we the readers are **taken by surprise**. The sudden change is shocking for us in a similar way to the surprise felt by the soldiers.

This is a very effective and memorable war poem because it focuses on a specific time and place. It is not a poem I took pleasure from, but the 'shady lane', 'shining canal' and 'blue' sky give me a clear picture of the place before the battle happens.

COMMENT

- The student **shows how** the **setting** contributes to the **mood or atmosphere** in the poem.
- In the second paragraph, the importance of the **setting is developed** through exploration of **contrasting descriptions** of the same **location**.
- The entire answer is well supported by **quotation of key words** from the poem.

Sample exam paper

SECTION 2: POETRY (60 marks)

Read the following poem by Pakistani poet, Imtiaz Dharker, in which she celebrates the importance of water to a community, and answer the questions which follow.

Blessing

Imtiaz Dharker

The skin cracks like a pod.
There never is enough water.

Imagine the drip of it,
the small splash, echo
in a tin mug,
the voice of a kindly god.

Sometimes, the sudden rush
of fortune. The municipal pipe bursts,
silver crashes to the ground
and the flow has found
a roar of tongues. From the huts,
a congregation: every man woman
child for streets around
butts in, with pots,
brass, copper, aluminium,
plastic buckets,
frantic hands,

and naked children
screaming in the liquid sun,
their highlights polished to perfection,
flashing light,
as the blessing sings
over their small bones.

* Municipal: Provided by the local council

Answer **QUESTION ONE and QUESTION TWO**

QUESTION ONE (30 marks)
Answer any **two** of the following questions. Each question is worth 15 marks.

1. From your reading of this poem, what do you learn about the people in it and the place where it is set? Support your answer with reference to the poem.
2. How does the poet convey a sense of excitement about the water in the poem?
3. Choose two of your favourite images relating to sound from this poem. Explain why you like these images.

QUESTION TWO (30 marks)
Answer **EITHER 1 OR 2** which follow.

N.B. In answering you may **NOT** use the poem given on this paper. You must give the title of the poem you choose and the name of the poet.

1. Select a poem you have studied which deals with either war **OR** peace.
   (i) What does the poet say about either war **or** peace in the poem?
   Support your answer by reference to the poem. (15 marks)
   (ii) What effect did this poem have on you?
   Explain your answer with reference to the poem. (15 marks)

OR

2. Poetry offers us a way to explore places we have never been, foreign lands and different cultures. Choose a poem you have studied which creates such a place.
   (i) Describe the place created in this poem.
   Support your answer with reference to the poem. (15 marks)
   (ii) Would you like to live there?
   Explain your answer with reference to the poem. (15 marks)

(2009, Paper 2, Section 2, Poetry)

7 Fiction

Read	Revised	Recapped

- To learn the skill of **close reading** stories.
- To identify **elements of storytelling**.
- To analyse **style and genre**.
- To examine **character, plot and style**

The Fiction section is the final section of Paper 2. You must answer one question on **Unseen Fiction and** one question on **Studied Fiction**. The questions carry equal marks.

Essentially you must apply the same **skills of close reading** needed for the **Reading** question on Paper 1 to the **Unseen Fiction** question on Paper 2. Marks are awarded for **relevant points** supported by **references to the text** and clearly **explained**.

You should:

1. Read the **story, highlighting key points**.
2. Read the **question**, identifying **key words** and **highlighting** them.
3. **List a variety of points** for each answer and try to **link** or connect these points.
4. **Divide the time available equally** between all parts of the question. Once your allotted time for answering a question has passed, move on to the next question.

Unseen fiction

All fiction involves **storytelling**. Sometimes there will be a **narrator** or storyteller who can be easily identified. If the character is telling his or her own story, it is a **first-person narrative**. If the character is referred to as 'he' or 'she', it is a **third-person narrative**. Occasionally a question will focus on the person telling the story, asking you to deal with the narrator's attitudes or feelings about another character or some aspect of the plot.

Plot

Many Fiction questions will require you to explain details of the **plot** or storyline in the narrative. You may be asked to clarify a sequence of events, the causes of an incident or the consequences of certain actions. Here it is important to **logically outline** the **connection between events** in a coherent way.

Characters

Another crucial aspect of fiction is **character**. Most Unseen Fiction questions will include a task related to the characters in the story. You might be asked to examine the **nature of a** character, their **behaviour** or **outlook**. Sometimes, questions centre on the **relationship between characters**: possibly some form of **conflict**, or even a simple **contrast** between the actions and attitudes of characters in a narrative text.

Style

A slightly more complex task is a question related to the **writer's technique**. Sometimes you will be asked to dwell on the author's **style**, the overall **tone or atmosphere** of a story, or the ways in which a writer **achieves this effect**. In questions of style, your answer must **focus** on the **words and phrases** used in the passage in order to support your views.

Prose fiction

You may be asked for **your response** to a piece of prose fiction. Here, the emphasis is on **you as a young reader**. You should always **be aware** of the **feelings and ideas** the story **evokes** in you.

Your judgement of the quality of a story is influenced by other novels and stories you have read. Before the exam, you must **give some thought to the types of story you enjoy** and ask yourself **why** you like these stories. Perhaps you enjoy romances, thrillers or fantasy adventures. Your knowledge and experience **as a reader** is very relevant to the answers you give in this section of the exam.

Plot, character and **style** are the main features of fiction.

A   Read the extract below and answer the questions that follow.

Background to the text
Bog Child is set near the Republic of Ireland–Northern Ireland border in 1981. Fergus McCann is a teenage boy who lives in Northern Ireland during the Troubles.

Bog Child

Siobhan Dowd

They'd stolen a march on the day. The sky was like dark glass, reluctant to let the light through. The only sound was the chudder of the van skirting the lough. The surface of the water was colourless. The hills slumped down on the far side like silhouettes of snoozing giants.

Fergus yawned. It was still before five as they turned off up the mountain road. Uncle Tally chewed on nothing

bog child
SIOBHAN DOWD

as the tyres lumbered over the ruts. Fergus cradled the flask of sweet black tea. There'd been no milk in the fridge that morning.

'Too early for you, huh?' mocked Uncle Tally, changing gear.

'Too right,' said Fergus. 'When I go running, it's not dark like this.' His throat was furred up. The words came out stretched by a yawn. 'It's unnatural being up before the birds.'

They approached the border checkpoint and the van slowed. The soldier by the hut stood with a rifle but did not move. He was young-looking and pale, with freckles. He waved them on, tipping the butt of the gun, and they drove past without having to stop. Uncle Tally laughed. 'I could have a truckload of Semtex for all that wee squaddie cares,' he said.

Fergus grunted. 'Yeah,' he said. 'Deus would be delighted.'

Deus, Latin for 'God', was the local nickname for a rumoured bomb-maker, said to be active thereabouts.

'So he would.'

'Only you'd be going in the wrong direction. We're leaving the Troubles, Unk, not joining them.'

Uncle Tally thumped the wheel. 'So we are. We're in the free state now. Free as a bloody bog-frog.' They both laughed like clowns. Going over the border always had that effect. Without your knowing it, your jaw-bone would stiffen and adrenalin pump through your veins as the checkpoint approached. Then, when you were through, hilarity would erupt at the relief.

The van turned up onto a steep road with grass growing up the middle. The gorse got yellower as they climbed, the sky brighter. 'The border. Even a nun would be nervous crossing it,' suggested Fergus.

'And we'll be crossing back over it at the top.'

'Will we?'

'If you look at the map. You can see.'

Fergus opened the map and saw the dotted grey line, almost invisible, meandering across Ireland's north, but leaving a thin tract of land to the west that was Donegal. 'The most northern bit of Ireland's in the south,' he quoted.

'One day, one day . . .' Uncle Tally muttered like a mantra.

'One day what?'

'One day the only border will be the sea and the only thing guarding it the dunes and the only people living in it Republicans. One day, Fergus.'

'Where will the Unionists go, so?'

'They'll be beamed to outer space, warp factor five.' Uncle Tally drove round a loop of road, heading back to where the light was growing on the horizon. 'Lucky them. Now, here's the spot to park, Fergus. Get cracking. The JCB crew will be down on us before you know.'

He pulled up and they got out the shovels and bags from the back and walked over a track for a hundred yards. On either side, brown grass sprouted out of black, wet earth, and bright green weeds spread like mildew over the soggier areas. The first skylark of the day darted from cover. Fergus approached the JCB, which was still, abandoned. Earth was churned up all around it, the leftover diggings from the day before. But 'earth' was the wrong word. It was turf, rich foaming peat, made from the things that had lived here in millennia gone by and pressed by time into a magic frieze of the past. You could dig up wood from primeval forests, find resin with insects of another age frozen in it. And what you dug up you could burn as fuel.

And, as his da said, there was nothing like the smell of the turf on a hearth to bring comfort in a dark world.

A pink tint grew on the horizon as they dug and filled the bags with uncut clumps. Dawn intensified. The sky was clear and close up here, the mind uncluttered. Uncle Tally grunted as he shovelled, his taut, fit frame enjoying the work. Fergus held the bags open for him and then they swapped over. They'd sell the bags for ninety pence and Fergus was promised a cut of thirty per cent. But the JCB crew would be arriving soon and they'd have to be well gone by then.

A cry made Fergus swivel round. It was only a wild kid with a creamy coat, bleating at its mother fifty yards away or more.

'Get the flask, Fergus,' Uncle Tally said. 'I'm parched. I'd a skinful last night.'

'Did you?'

'Yes. Your da and Pad McGuire. They came down to Finicule's for one. And you know how it is.'

'Were you singing, Unk?'

'We were so far gone we were singing "Three Blind Mice". I ask you. And your da couldn't get beyond "See how they run". And it was only ten o'clock.'

'I don't believe you.'

'OK. Maybe not quite so wild.'

Fergus went to the van and found the flask of tea. He brought it over and they strolled down to an outcrop of rock and shared a capful. The rim of the sun came over the mountain. A wind picked up.

'Christ, it's quiet up here,' said Uncle Tally.

'It'd be a strange place to live.'

'You'd have to be a hermit.'

'There'd be nothing to do but pray,' said Fergus.

'Aye. You'd have plenary indulgences made for every last sinner by the time you died yourself. And then you'd be whisked up straight to heaven.'

'You should move up here.'

'I would too. Only it's a bit far.'

'Far from where?'

'The nearest bar.'

'You could make your own distillery, Unk.'

'But what would you distil?'

'The prayers. What else?'

Uncle Tally clipped his ear. 'You're too sharp, Fergus McCann. Pass me the flask.'

After tea, they filled another ten bags. When there was no loosened turf left, Uncle Tally left the shovel prodded into the earth and they began to load the bags into the van.

'Not a bad haul.'

Fergus wandered off to the other side of the JCB. He watched the skyline and listened to morning getting under way. There was a hum of insects now, small movements of birds and, far off from the floor of the valley, the sound of the odd truck. The sun was up, white and smooth behind a whisper of cloud. The track led back to the road, and the road truncated the bog-land and headed straight to the horizon. Up here was borderland too. He was looking back into the North, but behind him was the Republic.

'Ferg, shake a leg,' called Uncle Tally.

'Will we do another few bags?'

'What time is it?'

Fergus looked at the watch he was minding for his older brother, Joe. 'Not seven yet.'

'OK. But we've to make a fresh cut of it.'

A shovel apiece, they scrambled into the cut the JCB had made last thing the day before.

'You work that end, I'll work this. You've to ram the sharp side in straight and up in a line.' Uncle Tally showed him how. 'Then down along.'

'Like a grid?'

'That's it. Once you've the first line out, it's easier.' It was slower going than working with the JCB's leavings. But the smell of the fresh peat was clean and the springy consistency strangely satisfying to cut into.

Fergus finished a good-sized grid and worked down along the cut, away from his uncle.

'Hiyack!' he shouted as he brought the shovel hard down at a fresh angle. One inch from the wall of brown turf, he froze. A foreign colour stopped him, a dull, tawny glint. He let the shovel topple at his side and his eyes blinked. Then he stretched out a hand to touch the surface. Maybe it was a trick of the light. Or a stone. Or—

Questions

Answer **two** of the following questions. Each question is worth 15 marks.

1. Describe the setting of this story.
2. How does the writer introduce the characters of Fergus and Uncle Tally?
3. Do you think this is an interesting opening scene for a teenage novel? Explain your answer.

Always **highlight** the **key words** in a question.

Setting refers to the **unique time and place** in which a story happens. Settings can create **atmosphere**.

Hints for approaching these questions

1. The setting of a story is the **time** or era and the **location** in which the story takes place. Look carefully at the **background to the extract** for important information about the setting. There are references to the **Troubles**, a period of time in Northern Ireland when there was frequent loss of life because of political violence.

   The extract includes information about a **checkpoint and soldiers**, which links to the background reference to the Troubles. Uncle Tally and Fergus also talk about **bombs and explosives** and this indicates a setting where violence is a regular feature of life.

   In contrast to this violence are the details of **natural or scenic beauty** in the opening pages of the novel. Your answer should make reference to the **physical place** where the story is set. The **bog** of the title is described in great detail. There are many references to the weather, landscape, plants and wildlife of the bog.

   Finally, this setting is a **workplace**. The bog is a place where Fergus and his Uncle go to work, even if their work is stealing turf! The details of the **machinery** used to harvest the turf help to establish that this is a place where people are busy making a living from the land.

2. There is a great deal of **dialogue** in the opening pages of *Bog Child*. It is used to reveal the characters and the relationship between them. They chat about the place, their work, the Troubles and going to the pub. All of this gives us a sense of characters with a variety of concerns and interests.

   The dialogue also shows us that Uncle Tally is in charge and Fergus is his helper. **Tally gives orders** and instructions to his young assistant.

   When they speak, their language is **colloquial**. The writer makes the characters real by giving them intimate, familiar language when they speak to each other. What they say also tells us about their **attitudes** to the place, their work, the conflict in the North and drinking!

3. The third question asks for your **own response** to the novel. It is aimed at a **teenage audience** and you are expected to say, from your reading of the opening scene, whether or not teenagers would find it interesting.

A good answer would discuss some of the following:

- **Setting**: Are the time and place of interest to you? Why or why not?
- **Characters**: Do Tally and Fergus engage your interest or curiosity?
- **Situation**: Does the mystery at the end of the extract arouse your interest? You must explain why or why not, with reference to the passage.
- **Style**: Do you find the writer's use of words enjoyable, original or stimulating? State why or why not, with reference to the text.

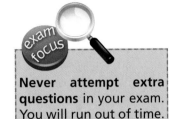

exam focus

Never attempt extra questions in your exam. You will run out of time.

exam Q

B Read the short story below and answer the questions that follow.

The Dragon Ring of Connla

Patricia Lynch

Cuchulain had only one son and, after he had finished his own training with Scatha in the Land of Shadows, he left a ring for the child and asked that he should be called Connla.

'Train him as you trained me,' he said. 'When he has grown big enough for it to fit his finger, give him the ring. And let him be under *geis* (bond) not to make himself known, never to turn out of the way for any man and never to refuse a fight!'

Years later, when Cuchulain had become a great champion, King Conor of Ulster and some of his warriors were gathered on the shore, when they saw a boat coming over the sea.

'That's a strange boat!' exclaimed Conor. 'Can it be made of bronze?'

Sunlight gleamed on the boat, on the golden oars and on the fair hair of the boy who rode towards them. Presently he pulled in the oars and, while the boat drifted landwards on the tide, he took up his sling, chose a stone from a heap lying before him and cast at a sea bird flying overhead, so that it fell alive at his feet.

'I wonder where that lad comes from!' muttered Conor. 'If he can fight as well as he casts, the men of his country must be great warriors. If they invaded Ulster, we'd be destroyed. Go down Condery; warn him to keep away.' As the boat drew in, Condery strode to the edge of the sea and shouted to the stranger not to come ashore. 'I'm going to land at this very spot!' declared the boy. 'I'll not turn back for you or anyone!'

He leaped from the boat, thrust it off with his spear and splashed up the strand.

Conall of the Victories, amazed that Condery had allowed the boy to leave the boat, marched down to them. Before he came within speaking distance, the young stranger picked up the largest stone he could see and hurled it at the warrior. Conall fell senseless and, while he lay unconscious, the boy ran over to him and bound his arms.

Condery, who was unarmed, retreated and another warrior went to subdue the young hero, but he was no luckier than Conall.

King Conor was angry. He strode to a rocky ledge above the strand and hailed the boy.

'What is your name, who is your father and where do you come from?'

'I'll not tell you!' shouted the lad. 'And I'll not go from this place if you bring your whole army against me.'

The warriors had begun by laughing at his boastfulness. Now, as Ulsterman after Ulsterman was attacked and beaten, shame made Conor furious.

'Go to Cuchulain,' he said, 'and tell him to come down to the strand and fight with the stranger, who is defeating all our warriors, even Conall of the Victories.'

Cuchulain was at home in Dundalk with Emer his wife, when the messenger came.

'Conor has a whole army, yet he must send for you!' she cried indignantly.

But Cuchulain was hanging his shield over his arm and taking down his sword and spear.

'If Conor sends for me, I'd be disgraced for ever if I didn't go!' he declared.

Emer knew that and was proud of him. But she was troubled and there was no smile on her face as he leaped into his chariot.

Cuchulain drove to where Conor and his men watched the fair boy tossing javelins into the air and catching them in order, one by one while, on the sand, lay a row of bound warriors, helpless and ashamed.

'Do you ask me to fight a boy?' Cuchulain asked Conor.

'I do!' replied the king. 'But I would sooner have him among my own warriors. Go against him, for there lies Conall of the Victories and six more of our best fighters, bound at the mercy of this young barbarian!'

'This is strange!' said Cuchulain. 'There is no boy of his age or size in Ireland could put Conall on his back. I must know more of this lad.'

He went along the strand and the boy smiled at him, still tossing his weapons and catching them easily.

'What is your name, my lad?' asked Cuchulain. 'And where do you come from?'

'I can't tell you that!' replied the boy.

'A pity!' said Cuchulain. 'For then you must die.'

'If I die, I die!' declared the strange lad. He flung down his javelins and taking his sword, went to meet Cuchulain.

The champion did not fight seriously, for he was determined not to harm the boy. But when a lock of his hair was shorn off, he knew he must treat his opponent as a real warrior.

'We'll have no more play!' he thought.

Cuchulain was using all his strength and skill, yet he could not drive that boy back one inch. He planted himself upon a rock and stood so firmly his feet sank into the stone and, to this day, that place is called the Strand of the Footprints.

The boy was growing tired but, with a swift turn, he gripped Cuchulain by the arm. As the Champion tried to free himself, they both toppled into the sea. Cuchulain was underneath and was drowning when he remembered the Gáe Bolg. He had brought the terrible body spear with him, though he had not dreamed he would need to use it. Now he thrust it at the boy and the barbs pierced his limbs.

'I am hurt!' he cried. 'Why didn't Scatha teach me that?'

Cuchulain dragged him from the water and stretched him on the sand. The setting sun struck a flash from a ring on the boy's finger – a ring in the form of a dragon with emerald eyes, biting its own tail. Cuchulain knew the ring. He lifted the lad in his arms and laid him before Conor and the warriors.

'Here is my only son, Connla, that I have killed for you, men of Ulster!' he said.

'It is true, I am Connla!' agreed the boy. 'If only I had a few years to train among you, Cuchulain and I would have led you against the world. I thought I had years before me, but as my death has come, show me the famous warriors and let me say goodbye to them.'

Conall of the Victories, who had been set free, and the other famous men knelt and kissed him while Cuchulain stood weeping.

Then Connla died and over his grave they carved a pillar stone with the story of his short life. He was the only son Cuchulain ever had and he killed him for the honour of Ulster.

Questions

1. What is **ironic** about Cuchulain's instructions to Scatha? (10 marks)
2. This is an old Irish **legend**. Identify and comment on the characteristics of this style of storytelling. (10 marks)
3. Which character in the story do you sympathise with most? (10 marks)

key point

Legends are stories passed down from ancient times, involving superhuman or heroic deeds and mythical creatures.

key point

Irony is when there is a **contrast** between **what a character says or does** and **reality**. In this story, Cuchulain issues instructions believing that they will help his son. Ironically, his son dies because he follows those same instructions.

SAMPLE ANSWERS

ANSWER 1

First of all, Cuchulain leaves a ring with Scatha to give to his child. He asks for the boy to be named 'Connla'. The 'ring in the shape of the dragon' was later one of the **clues** that revealed the boy's identity to his father.

It is deeply **ironic** that, having named his own child, Cuchulain is forced to ask him 'What is your name, my lad?' Of course this would never have happened if Cuchulain had not told Scatha to put Connla 'under *geis* (bond) not to make himself known'. Clearly he felt it was necessary to give the boy a degree of anonymity growing up as son of the Champion of Ulster. **If he had known the boy's name, he never would have fought him.**

The instruction 'never to turn out of the way for any man' was another mistake because the boy obediently followed this in refusing to submit to any of King Conor's men. **If he had not been instructed to be so uncompromising, his tragic death could have been avoided.** Ironically, his own father helped to bring this about.

Cuchulain's final request was to teach his son **'never to refuse a fight'**. This was the last straw in the boy's defeat, as he was under obligation to fight his own father because he was expected to bravely confront any enemy.

COMMENT

- **Irony** is the **gap between what is said** and **what is true** or real.
- All the **irony** here rests on the fact that **Cuchulain does not know Connla's identity**.
- In this answer, the **ironic impact** of Cuchulain's instructions to Scatha and the failure of the men of Ulster to recognise the boy are **clearly explained**.

ANSWER 2

The story begins in 'the Land of Shadows'. Myths or legends are often set in a distant time or place. The **names** of the characters (Scatha, King Conor and Conall of the Victories) are not like ordinary modern names, as they imply **mystery**, **royalty** and **heroism** in battle.

Another feature of legends is characters with **superhuman power**. Connla, while still a mere boy, can fight and defeat a host of grown warriors who have already proven themselves in battle. His father has the power of a superhero, too, since he gains victory over Connla using the 'Gáe Bolg'. This 'terrible body spear' is not a normal weapon but clearly has some **magical power**.

Legends usually involve **heroic** acts of bravery, battles and **tragic** death. There are several examples of courage from Condery to Cuchulain and Connla himself. The scene on the strand that day must have looked like a battle, as the beach was covered with warriors 'bound at the mercy of this young barbarian'. Sadly the story includes a shocking death when Connla is killed by his own father.

One last detail that is common to myths and legends is the explanation of the name the Strand of the Footprints. In the midst of the story, we learn that the beach got its name from the marks of Cuchulain's feet left on a rock during his struggle with Connla.

COMMENT
- Various **features** of the legend are identified in the story.
- Each point is illustrated well by means of a **quotation**.

Answer 3

I sympathise most with Connla in this story. He is the only one to lose his life; all of the other characters survive, even though some of them have been beaten, humiliated or wounded.

Connla also deserves sympathy because he was killed by a member of his own family. Usually your family protect you, but because of the strange circumstances, the opposite happens in this legend.

I feel sorry for the boy because, in trying to please his father by obeying his orders, he unwittingly brings about his own death. It must have been hard not to divulge his true identity and then to have to do battle with his own father.

A sad aspect of Connla's life is the fact that he grew up with Scatha and not with his family. I think Connla deserves to be pitied for all these reasons.

COMMENT
- This question requires the student to give their own **personal** response to the tragedy.
- In this answer, the candidate speaks in the **first person**, explaining how they **respond** to the character of Connla.

C   **Read the short story below and answer the questions that follow.**

The Ring

Bryan MacMahon

I should like you to have known my grandmother. She was my mother's mother, and as I remember her she was a widow with a warm farm in the Kickham country in Tipperary. Her land was on the southern slope of a hill, and there it drank in the sun which, to me, seemed always to be balanced on the teeth of the Galtees. Each year I spent the greater part of my summer holidays at my grandmother's place. It was a great change for me to leave our home in a bitter sea-coast village in Kerry and visit my grandmother's. Why, man, the grass gone to waste on a hundred yards on the roadside in Tipperary was as much as you'd find in a dozen of our sea-poisoned fields. I always thought it a pity to see all that fine grass go to waste by the verge of the road. I think so still.

Although my Uncle Con was married, my grandmother held the whip hand in the farm. At the particular time I am trying to recall, the first child was in the cradle. (Ah, how time has galloped away! That child is now a nun in a convent on the Seychelles Islands.) My Uncle Con's wife, my Aunt Annie, was a gentle, delicate girl who was only charmed in herself to have somebody to assume the responsibility of the place. Which was just as well indeed, considering the nature of woman my grandmother was. Since that time when her husband's horse had walked into the farmyard unguided, with my grandfather, Martin Dermody, dead in the body of the car, her heart had turned to stone in her breast. Small wonder to that turning, since she was left with six young children – five girls and one boy, my Uncle Con. But she faced the world bravely and did well by them all. Ah! But she was hard, main hard.

Once at a race-meeting I picked up a jockey's crop. When I balanced it on my palm it reminded me of my grandmother. Once I had a twenty-two pound salmon laced to sixteen feet of Castleconnell greenheart; the rod reminded me of my grandmother. True, like crop and rod, she had an element of flexibility, but like them there was no trace of fragility. Now after all those years I cannot recall her person clearly; to me she is but something tall and dark and austere. But lately I see things that puzzled me when I was a boy. Towards me she displayed a certain black affection. Oh, but I made her laugh warmly once. That was when I told her of the man who had stopped me on the road beyond the limekiln and asked me if I were a grandson of Martin Dermody. Inflating with a shy pride, I had told him that I was. He then gave me a shilling and said, 'Maybe you're called Martin after your grandfather?' 'No,' I said, 'I'm called Con after my Uncle Con.' It was then my grandmother had laughed a little warmly. But my Uncle Con caught me under the armpits, tousled my hair and said I was a clever Kerry rascal.

The solitary occasion on which I remember her to have shown emotion was remarkable. Maybe remarkable isn't the proper word; obscene would be closer to the mark. Obscene I would have thought of it then, had I known the meaning of the word.

Today I think it merely pathetic.

How was it that it all started? Yes, there was I with my bare legs trailing from the heel of a loaded hay-float. I was watching the broad silver parallels we were leaving in the clean after-grass. My Uncle Con was standing in the front of the float guiding the mare. Drawing in the hay to the hayshed we were. Already we had a pillar and a half of the hayshed filled. My grandmother was up on the hay, forking the lighter trusses. The servant-boy was handling the heavier forkfuls. A neighbour was throwing it up to them.

When the float stopped at the hayshed I noticed that something was amiss. For one thing the man on the hay was idle, as indeed was the man on the ground. My grandmother was on the ground, looking at the hay with cold calculating eyes. She turned to my Uncle Con.

'Draw in no more hay, Con,' she said. 'I've lost my wedding ring.'

'Where? In the hay?' he queried.

'Yes, in the hay.'

'But I thought you had a keeper?'

'I've lost the keeper too. My hands are getting thin.'

'The story could be worse,' he commented.

My grandmother did not reply for a little while. She was eyeing the stack with enmity.

''Tis in that half-pillar,' she said at last. 'I must look for it.'

'You've a job before you, mother,' said Uncle Con.

She spoke to the servant-boy and the neighbour. 'Go down and shake out those couple of pikes at the end of the Bog Meadow,' she ordered. 'They're heating in the centre.'

'Can't we be drawing in to the idle pillar, mother?' my Uncle Con asked gently.

'No, Con,' she answered. 'I'll be putting the hay from the middle pillar there.'

The drawing-in was over for the day. That was about four o'clock in the afternoon. Before she tackled the half-pillar my grandmother went down on her hands and knees and started to search the loose hay in the idle pillar. She searched wisp by wisp, even sop by sop. My Uncle Con beckoned to me to come away. Anyway, we knew she'd stop at six o'clock. 'Six to six' was her motto for working hours. She never broke that rule.

That was a Monday evening. On Tuesday we offered to help – my Uncle Con and I. She was down on her hands and knees when we asked her. 'No, no,' she said abruptly. Then, by way of explanation, when she saw that we were crestfallen: 'You see, if we didn't find it I'd be worried that ye didn't search as carefully as ye should, and I'd have no peace of mind until I had searched it all over again.' So she worked hard all day, breaking off only for her meals and stopping sharp at six o'clock.

By Wednesday evening she had made a fair gap in the hay but had found no ring.

Now and again during the day we used to go down to see if she had had any success. She was very wan in the face when she stopped in the evening.

On Thursday morning her face was still more strained and drawn. She seemed reluctant to leave the rick even to take her meals. What little she ate seemed like so much dust in her mouth. We took down tea to her several times during the day.

By Friday the house was on edge. My Uncle Con spoke guardedly to her at dinnertime.

'This will set us back a graydle, mother,' he said. 'I know, son: I know, son: I know,' was all she said in reply.

Saturday came and the strain was unendurable. About three o'clock in the afternoon she found the keeper. We had been watching her in turns from the kitchen window. I remember my uncle's face lighting up and his saying, 'Glory, she's found it!' But he drew a long breath when again she started burrowing feverishly in the hay. Then we knew it was only the keeper. We didn't run out at all. We waited till she came in at six o'clock. There were times between three and six when our three heads were together at the small window watching her. I was thinking she was like a mouse nibbling at a giant's loaf.

At six she came in and said, 'I found the keeper.' After her tea she couldn't stay still. She fidgeted around the kitchen for an hour or so. Then, 'Laws were made to be broken,' said my grandmother with brittle bravery, and she stalked out to the hayshed. Again we watched her.

Coming on for dusk she returned and lighted a stable lantern and went back to resume her search. Nobody crossed her. We didn't say yes aye or no to her. After a time my Uncle Con took her heavy coat off the rack and went down and threw it across her shoulders. I was with him. 'There's a touch of frost here tonight, mother,' said my Uncle Con.

We loitered for a while in the darkness outside the ring of her lantern's light. But she resented our pitying eyes so we went in. We sat around the big fire waiting – Uncle Con, Aunt Annie and I. That was the lonely waiting – without speaking – just as if we were waiting for an old person to die or for a child to come into the world. Near twelve we heard her step on the cobbles. 'Twas typical of my grandmother that she placed the lantern on the ledge of the dresser and quenched the candle in it before she spoke to us.

'I found it,' she said. The words dropped out of her drawn face.

'Get hot milk for my mother, Annie,' said Uncle Con briskly.

My grandmother sat by the fire, a little to one side. Her face was as cold as death. I kept watching her like a hawk but her eyes didn't even flicker. The wedding ring was inside its keeper, and my grandmother kept twirling it round and round with the fingers of her right hand.

Suddenly, as if ashamed of her fingers' betrayal, she hid her hands under her check apron. Then, unpredictably, the fists under the apron came up to meet her face, and her face bent down to meet the fists in the apron. 'Oh, Martin, Martin,' she sobbed, and then she cried like the rain.

D Read the extract below and answer the questions that follow.

Background to the novel

In the novel *Jane Eyre*, the eponymous heroine is an orphan who escapes her cruel Aunt Reed only to suffer further hardship at the Lowood Institution, a home for orphaned children. Here she meets a kind mentor, Miss Temple, and befriends another girl called Helen Burns. In the extract below, Jane leaves her own dormitory late at night to visit her friend, who is being treated for a serious illness and is kept in isolation in Miss Temple's room.

Always read the **background to the extract** for vital clues about the story and characters.

Jane Eyre

Charlotte Brontë

It might be two hours later, probably near eleven, when I – not having been able to fall asleep, and deeming, from the perfect silence of the dormitory, that my companions were all wrapt in profound repose – rose softly, put on my frock over my night-dress, and, without shoes, crept from the apartment, and set off in quest of Miss Temple's room. It was quite at the other end of the house; but I knew my way; and the light of the unclouded summer moon, entering here and there at passage windows, enabled me to find it without difficulty. An odour of camphor and burnt vinegar warned me when I came near the fever room: and I passed its door quickly, fearful lest the nurse who  sat up all night should hear me. I dreaded being discovered and sent back; for I must see Helen, – I must embrace her before she died, – I must give her one last kiss, exchange with her one last word.

Having descended a staircase, traversed a portion of the house below, and succeeded in opening and shutting, without noise, two doors, I reached another flight of steps; these I mounted, and then just opposite to me was Miss Temple's room. A light shone through the keyhole and from under the door; a profound stillness pervaded the vicinity. Coming near, I found the door slightly ajar; probably to admit some fresh air into the close abode of sickness. Indisposed to hesitate, and full of impatient impulses – soul and senses quivering with keen throes – I put it back and looked in. My eye sought Helen, and feared to find death.

Close by Miss Temple's bed, and half covered with its white curtains, there stood a little crib. I saw the outline of a form under the clothes, but the face was hid by the hangings: the nurse I had spoken to in the garden sat in an easy-chair asleep; an unsnuffed candle burnt dimly on the table. Miss Temple was not to be seen: I knew afterwards that she had been called to a delirious patient in the fever-room. I advanced; then paused by the crib side: my hand was on the curtain, but I preferred speaking before I withdrew it. I still recoiled at the dread of seeing a corpse.

'Helen,' I whispered softly, 'are you awake?'

She stirred herself, put back the curtain, and I saw her face, pale, wasted, but quite composed: she looked so little changed that my fear was instantly dissipated.

'Can it be you, Jane?' she asked, in her own gentle voice.

'Oh!' I thought, 'she is not going to die; they are mistaken: she could not speak and look so calmly if she were.'

I got on to her crib and kissed her: her forehead was cold, and her cheek both cold and thin, and so were her hand and wrist; but she smiled as of old.

'Why are you come here, Jane? It is past eleven o'clock: I heard it strike some minutes since.'

'I came to see you, Helen: I heard you were very ill, and I could not sleep till I had spoken to you.'

'You came to bid me good-bye, then: you are just in time probably.'

'Are you going somewhere, Helen? Are you going home?'

'Yes; to my long home – my last home.'

'No, no, Helen!' I stopped, distressed. While I tried to devour my tears, a fit of coughing seized Helen; it did not, however, wake the nurse; when it was over, she lay some minutes exhausted; then she whispered –

'Jane, your little feet are bare; lie down and cover yourself with my quilt.'

I did so: she put her arm over me, and I nestled close to her. After a long silence, she resumed, still whispering –

'I am very happy, Jane; and when you hear that I am dead, you must be sure and not grieve: there is nothing to grieve about. We all must die one day, and the illness which is removing me is not painful; it is gentle and gradual: my mind is at rest. I leave no one to regret me much: I have only a father; and he is lately married, and will not miss me. By dying young, I shall escape great sufferings. I had not qualities or talents to make my way very well in the world: I should have been continually at fault.'

'But where are you going to, Helen? Can you see? Do you know?'

'I believe; I have faith: I am going to God.'

'Where is God? What is God?'

'My Maker and yours, who will never destroy what He created. I rely implicitly on His power, and confide wholly in His goodness: I count the hours till that eventful one arrives which shall restore me to Him, reveal Him to me.'

'You are sure, then, Helen, that there is such a place as heaven, and that our souls can get to it when we die?'

'I am sure there is a future state; I believe God is good; I can resign my immortal part to Him without any misgiving. God is my father; God is my friend: I love Him; I believe He loves me.'

'And shall I see you again, Helen, when I die?'

'You will come to the same region of happiness: be received by the same mighty, universal Parent, no doubt, dear Jane.'

Again I questioned, but this time only in thought. 'Where is that region? Does it exist?'

And I clasped my arms closer round Helen; she seemed dearer to me than ever; I felt as if I could not let her go; I lay with my face hidden on her neck. Presently she said, in the sweetest tone –

'How comfortable I am! That last fit of coughing has tired me a little; I feel as if I could sleep: but don't leave me, Jane; I like to have you near me.'

'I'll stay with you, *dear* Helen: no one shall take me away.'

'Are you warm, darling?'

'Yes.'

'Good-night, Jane.'

'Good-night, Helen.'

She kissed me, and I her, and we both soon slumbered.

When I awoke it was day: an unusual movement roused me; I looked up; I was in somebody's arms; the nurse held me; she was carrying me through the passage back to the dormitory. I was not reprimanded for leaving my bed; people had something else to think about; no explanation was afforded then to my many questions; but a day or two afterwards I learned that Miss Temple, on returning to her own room at dawn, had found me laid in the little crib; my face against Helen Burns's shoulder, my arms round her neck. I was asleep, and Helen was – dead.

Her grave is in Brocklebridge churchyard: for fifteen years after her death it was only covered by a grassy mound; but now a grey marble tablet marks the spot, inscribed with her name, and the word '*Resurgam*'.

Questions

1. Describe the relationship between these two girls.
   (10 marks)

2. There is great sadness in this passage but also some hope of consolation for Jane. Do you agree with this statement? Explain with reference to the text.
   (10 marks)

3. Imagine you are Miss Temple. Write a diary extract based on the events outlined above.   (10 marks)

Diary entries should be **dated** and written in the **first person**.

E   **Read the extract below and answer the questions that follow.**

Circle of Friends

Maeve Binchy

1949

The kitchen was full of the smells of baking. Benny put down her school bag and went on a tour of inspection.

'The cake hasn't been iced yet,' Patsy explained. 'The mistress will do that herself.'

'What are you going to put on it?' Benny was eager.

'I suppose Happy Birthday Benny.' Patsy was surprised.

'Maybe she'll put Benny Hogan, Ten.'

'I never saw that on a cake.'

'I think it is, when it's a big birthday like being ten.'

'Maybe.' Patsy said doubtful.

'And are the jellies made?'

'They're in the pantry. Don't go in poking them, you'll leave the mark of your finger and we'll all be killed.'

'I can't believe I'm going to be ten,' Benny said, delighted with herself.

'Ah, it's a big day all right.' Patsy spoke absently as she greased the trays for the queen cakes with a scrap of butter paper.

'What did you do when you were ten?

'Don't you know with me every day was the same,' Patsy said cheerfully. 'There was no day different in the orphanage until I came out of it and came here.'

Benny loved to hear stories of the orphanage. She thought it was better than anything she read in books. There was the room with the twelve iron beds in it, the nice girls, the terrible girls, the time they all got nits in their hair and had to have their heads shaved.

'They must have had birthdays,' Benny insisted.

'I don't remember them,' Patsy sighed. 'There was a nice nun who said to me that I was Wednesday's child, full of woe.'

'That wasn't nice.'

'Well, at least she knew I was born on a Wednesday . . . Here's your mother, now let me get on with the work.'

Annabel Hogan came in carrying three big bags. She was surprised to see her daughter sitting swinging her legs in the kitchen.

'Aren't you home nice and early? Let me put these things upstairs.'

Benny ran over to Patsy when her mother's heavy tread was heard on the stairs.

'Do you think she got it?'

'Don't ask me, Benny, I know nothing.'

'You're saying that because you *do* know.

'I *don't*. Really.'

'Was she in Dublin? Did she go up on the bus?'

'No, not at all.'

'But she must have.' Benny seemed very disappointed.

'No, she's not long gone at all . . . She was only up the town.'

Benny licked the spoon thoughtfully. 'It's nicer raw,' she said.

'You always thought that.' Patsy looked at her fondly.

'When I'm eighteen and can do what I like, I'll eat all my cakes uncooked,' Benny pronounced.

'No you won't, when you're eighteen you'll be so busy getting thin you won't eat cakes at all.'

'I'll always want cakes.'

'You say that now. Wait till you want some fellow to fancy you.'

'Do you want a fellow to fancy you?'

'Of course I do, what else is there?'

'What fellow? I don't want you to go, anyway.'

'I won't get a fellow, I'm from nowhere, a decent fellow wouldn't be able to talk about me and where I came from. I have no background, no life before, you see.'

'But you had a *great* life,' Benny cried. 'You'd make them all interested in you.'

There was no time to discuss it further. Benny's mother was back in the kitchen, her coat off and down to business with the icing sugar.

'Were you in Dublin at all today, Mother?'

'No, child, I had enough to do getting things ready for the party.'

'It's just I was wondering . . .'

'Parties don't run themselves, you know.' The words sounded sharp but the tone was kindly. Benny knew her mother was looking forward to it all too.

'And will Father be home for the cake bit?'

'Yes, he will. We've asked the people for half-past three, they'll all be here by four, so we needn't sit down to the tea until half-past five, and we wouldn't have got to the cake until your father has the business closed, and is back here.'

Benny's father ran Hogan's Outfitters, the big menswear shop in the middle of Knockglen. The shop was often at its busiest on a Saturday, when the farmers came in, or the men who had a half day themselves were marched in by wives to have themselves fitted out by Mr Hogan, or Mike the old assistant, the tailor who had been there since time immemorial. Since the days when young Mr Hogan had bought the business.

Questions

1. Compare and contrast the characters of Benny and Patsy in this episode. (10 marks)

2. How would you describe the mood or atmosphere of this story? Explain your answer with close reference to the text. (10 marks)

3. This is the opening scene of a novel. Based on the passage above, do you think you would like to read this book? Explain your answer. (10 marks)

Mood is the **feeling** or **state of mind** created by a poem or story.

F **Read the extract below and answer the questions that follow.**

Background to the extract

Alex Rider, a fourteen-year-old superspy, has been sent by MI6 to investigate Point Blanc school, a mysterious institution high in the Alps owned by Dr Grief. In the following passage, Alex is fleeing the school on an improvised snowboard he has made from an ironing-board.

Point Blanc

Anthony Horowitz

Alex was on the edge of space, seemingly falling to certain death. In snowboarding language, he was catching air – meaning that he had shot away from the ground. Every ten metres he went forward, the mountainside disappeared another five metres downward. He felt the world spin around him. The wind whipped into his face. Then somehow he brought himself in line with the next section of the slope and shot down, steering the ironing-board ever

further from Point Blanc. He was moving at a terrifying speed, trees and rock formations passing in a luminous green blur across his night-vision goggles. In some ways the steeper slopes made it easier. At one point he had tried to make a landing on a flat part of the mountain – a tabletop – to slow himself down. He had hit the ground with such a bone-shattering crash that he had nearly blacked out and had taken the next twenty metres almost totally blind.

The ironing-board was shuddering and shaking crazily and it took all his strength to make the turns. He was trying to follow the natural fall-line of the mountain but there were too many obstacles in the way. What he most dreaded was melted snow. If the board landed on a patch of mud at this speed, he would be thrown and killed. And he knew that the further down he went, the greater the danger would become.

But he had been travelling for five minutes and so far he had only fallen twice – both times into thick banks of snow that had protected him. How far down could it be? He tried to remember what James Sprintz had told him, but thinking was impossible at this speed. He was having to use every ounce of his conscious thought simply to stay upright.

He reached a small lip where the surface was level and drove the edge of the board into the snow, bringing himself to a skidding halt. Ahead of him the ground fell away alarmingly. He hardly dared look down. There were thick clumps of trees to the left and to the right. In the distance there was just a green blur. The goggles could only see so far. And then he heard the noise coming up behind him. The scream of at least two – maybe more – engines. Alex looked back over his shoulder. For a moment there was nothing. But then he saw them – black flies swimming into his field of vision. There were two of them, heading his way.

Grief's men were riding specially adapted Yamaha Mountain Max snowmobiles equipped with 700cc triple-cylinder engines. The bikes were flying over the snow on their 141-inch tracks, effortlessly moving five times faster than Alex. The 300-watt headlights had already picked him out. Now the men sped towards him, cutting the distance between them with every second that passed.

Alex leapt forward, diving into the next slope. At the same moment, there was a sudden chatter, a series of distant cracks, and the snow leapt up all round him. Grief's men had machine-guns built into their snowmobiles! Alex yelled as he swooped down the mountainside, barely able to control the sheet of metal under his feet. The makeshift binding was tearing at his ankle. The whole thing was vibrating crazily. He couldn't see. He could only keep going, trying to keep his balance, hoping that the way ahead was clear.

The headlights of the nearest Yamaha shot out and Alex saw his own shadow stretch ahead of him on the snow. There was another chatter from the machine-gun and Alex ducked down, almost feeling the fan of bullets spray over his head. The second bike screamed up, coming parallel with him. He *had* to get off the mountainside. Otherwise he would be shot or run over. Or both.

He forced the board onto its edge, making a turn. He had seen a gap in the trees and he made for it. Now he was racing through the forest, with branches and trunks whipping past like crazy animations in a computer game. Could the snowmobiles follow him through here? The question was answered by another burst from the machine-guns, ripping through the leaves and branches. Alex searched for a narrower path. The board shuddered and he was almost thrown forward head first. The snow was getting thinner! He edged and turned, heading for two of the thickest trees. He passed between them with millimetres to spare. Now – follow that!

The Yamaha snowmobile had no choice. The rider had run out of paths. He was travelling too fast to stop. He tried to follow Alex between the trees, but the snowmobile was too wide. Alex heard a collision. There was a terrible crunch, then a scream, then an explosion. A ball of orange flame leapt over the trees, sending black shadows in a crazy dance. Ahead of him Alex saw another hillock and, beyond it, a gap in the trees. It was time to leave the forest.

He swooped up the hillock and out, once again catching air. As he left the trees behind him, two metres above the ground, he saw the second snowmobile. It had caught up with him. For a moment the two of them were side by side. Alex doubled forward and grabbed the nose of his board. Still in mid-air, he twisted the tip of the board, bringing the tail swinging round. He had timed it perfectly. The tail slammed into the second rider's head, almost throwing him out of his seat. The rider yelled and lost control. His snowmobile jerked sideways as if trying to make an impossibly tight turn. Then it left the ground, cartwheeling over and over again. The rider was thrown off, then screamed as the snowmobile completed its final turn and landed on top of him. Man and machine were bounced across the surface of the snow and then lay still. Alex slammed into the snow and skidded to a halt, his breath clouding green in front of his eyes.

Questions

1. What do you learn about Alex Rider in this passage?
   (10 marks)

2. Describe the conflict in this episode. How is this conflict resolved?
   (10 marks)

3. Anthony Horowitz is a popular children's writer. From your reading of this passage, can you account for his popularity? Explain your answer. (10 marks)

key point

Conflict is tension in a situation. The **resolution** is the final outcome of that conflict.

Studied fiction

The second part of the Fiction question will focus on the **novel** and **short stories** you have prepared in class with your teacher. **Plot**, **character**, **narrator** and the particular writing **style** of the author are the key areas to revise. Your answer should clearly **identify the title** of the novel or story and its **author**. Marks are awarded for

Revise your **novel** and at least one **short story**.

accurate focus on the question and for answers backed up with **precise detail** from the story. It is good but not essential to **quote** from the text; often a **specific reference** is sufficient for full marks.

Answer **EITHER 1 OR 2**.

1. Choose either the opening **or** the ending of a novel **or** short story you have studied.
   (a) Briefly describe what happens in the opening **or** the ending of your chosen text.
   (b) Did this opening **or** ending impress you? Explain your answer by reference to the novel **or** short story you have chosen.   (30 marks)

OR

2. From a novel **or** short story you have studied choose a character who experiences change.
   (a) Describe this character at the beginning of the novel **or** short story.
   (b) How has the character changed by the end of the novel **or** short story? Support your answer by reference to the text.   (30 marks)

(2005, Paper 2, Section 3, Fiction)

SAMPLE ANSWERS

ANSWER 2(a)

At the beginning of the novel *Of Mice and Men* by John Steinbeck we meet the **hero**, George. He is **described** as being 'small and quick, dark of face, with restless eyes and sharp, strong features'.

We realise that George is mentally the more **alert** of the two characters as his friend Lennie is almost like a child in his innocence and simplicity. George assumes **authority** as he orders 'Lennie, for God's sakes don't drink so much'. **This is how we learn that George is in charge and for the duration of the story this remains the case.**

We also find out that although George has assumed responsibility for Lennie he is growing **tired** of the trouble they get into together. He tells him he could 'get along so easy and so nice' if he didn't have to take care of Lennie.

The most **attractive** side of his personality is his ability to weave a dreamlike spell over an audience by telling a story. Lennie begs him to 'Tell how it's gonna be'. George then describes a utopian farm, a fantasy home for the pair of them. He paints a very attractive picture of a house where the two men could 'build up a fire in the stove and set around it an' listen to the rain comin' down on the roof'. This is their **dream**: a place of their own, where they will not be bothered by anyone, but instead enjoy simple comfort and security.

On the other hand, George is also **realistic** and, in anticipation of further trouble, tells Lennie to meet him at this spot if anything bad happens. This shows his ability to plan a strategy in order to avoid danger in the future.

COMMENT

- The answer begins with a physical **description** of George. His intelligence and sense of responsibility for Lennie's welfare are also explained with **evidence** from the story.
- **Additional points** deal with his storytelling ability and his awareness of the need for a plan to deal with any future trouble.

ANSWER 2(b)

At the end of the novel George is **still the wiser** of the two men. He is still well able to tell a story, as he uses the fantasy of their little farm with the rabbits to distract Lennie while he shoots him. His plan to meet at this spot should any trouble arise proves to be helpful, as Lennie has accidentally killed Curley's wife and has had to flee for his life.

The crucial **difference** in George is that he now realises there is no hope for Lennie. In the beginning, he thought they could overcome the problems they had in Weed by running away to work in a different part of the country. Now he knows there is no point in running. This time Lennie has broken the law in a fatal way. By killing Curley's wife he has endangered his own life. He will be killed either by Curley and Carlson, or later by execution for the crime of murder. George appreciates how serious this is, but Lennie cannot fully understand his predicament. For this reason, George reluctantly decides to kill his good friend.

George has changed in another key way. He now has had to **forsake his idyllic dream world**. The farm where he and George and possibly old Candy would live in harmony, feeding Lennie's rabbits and living off the 'fatta da lan'' will never come to pass. George's dream is not going to happen and instead of a peaceful future, he must face the awful prospect of Lennie being cruelly killed for the crime of murder.

Previously, when bad things happened George would give out to Lennie. At the end of the story, when they meet in the woods beside the Salinas river, Lennie asks him: 'Ain't you gonna give me hell?' This time there is no need for George to scold Lennie. George has **changed in his attitude towards his friend**; it is pointless to try to teach him how to behave in the future.

COMMENT

- A **clear comparison** is made between the **character** of George in the **opening scene** of the book and his attitudes and conduct at the **end**.
- Each **paragraph** makes a **new point** and **develops** it in a coherent way.

Key points to remember

For the Studied Fiction section, you must ensure that you revise **key details** of your novel and short story. Be very familiar with the following details:

- **Central characters**: heroes and villains.
- **Setting** of the story: time and place.
- Ideas explored by the writer: **themes**.
- **Key moments** in the story: opening scene, climax (confrontation) and resolution (ending) of the story.
- Your favourite **scene**.
- Your favourite **character**.
- Any **lesson** you learned and how it might be applied to your **own** experience.

If you have learned significant **quotations**, you should try to include them as support for your answer. However, full marks can still be attained once your answer makes **specific reference to key scenes** from the story.

Answer the question you are **asked**.

Sample exam paper

SECTION 3:   FICTION   (60 marks)

Read the extract below and then answer the questions which follow.

> The following extract is adapted from the novel *White Lies* by Mark O'Sullivan. The extract concerns a character referred to as OD, and his girlfriend, Nance.

OD

I loved weekend nights. I always had enough money to spend, and that made me feel I was better off out of school. If there was something to celebrate, like beating St Peter's and scoring the winner, it was even better. All night I'd never think that I'd be broke and wrecked in the morning.

For some reason I can't remember, our game was moved from Saturday to Sunday that weekend. After the match, I was up for a good time and Nance was being awkward. She made a habit of that. When I think about it, the reason I liked her and the reason she got on my nerves were basically the same. She had a mind of her own, a kind of cool, independent spirit that made her stand out from everyone else.

When she'd get on to me about leaving school and all that stuff, there was something cold and sarcastic about the way she talked. It was like she was warning me she wasn't going to hang around forever with someone who had no future. I hated that. I'd sort of cut my mind off and get thick. She had a way past that too. She'd make me feel like this mindless primitive, ready at any minute to lash out – even at her. It was true that there were a few people I wouldn't have minded belting; but that was all in my head, and I was sure it was going to stay there.

That business of me knocking over the phone was typical. The way she looked at me! You'd swear I'd meant to do it.

The funny thing was, I started going out with her just to get back at her father. I'd got on fine with him until things started to go wrong at home. I should say, when the things that were already wrong started coming out into the open. Tom Mahoney put the boot into me when I came in once too often with nothing done.

First day back in September, he lays it on the line for me. I had three weeks to prove to him I could take the Honours paper. Things got worse and at the end of the three weeks I said goodbye to the place. A week later, Mahoney took over as manager of the Youths team. I should have known then that you can't run away. That hating Mahoney was just an excuse.

So I asked Nance for a dance at a disco shortly after. I wasn't talking to her for more than five minutes before I'd forgotten all about Mahoney.

Before the night was out I'd told her everything. All that stuff about my folks and the hassle with Mahoney. She didn't lead me or ask questions, but somehow she drew it all out of me. It was like I'd been waiting for the right person to listen.

Answer QUESTION ONE and QUESTION TWO

QUESTION ONE   (30 marks)

Answer **two** of the following questions. Each question is worth 15 marks.

1. From your reading of this passage what impression of OD's life do you get?
2. What do we learn about the relationship between Nance and OD? Support your answer by reference to the extract.
3. Judging from what you have read in this extract, would you like to read more of this novel? Explain your answer with reference to the passage.

QUESTION TWO   (30 marks)

Answer **EITHER 1 OR 2** which follow.

1. Select a novel or short story you have studied which has an interesting theme.
   (i) Outline the theme of the text you have chosen.   (15 marks)
   (ii) As the theme develops why does it interest you?   (15 marks)
   Support your answer with reference to your chosen novel or short story.

OR

2. Choose a favourite section from a novel or short story you have studied.
   (i) Describe what happens in this section of your chosen text. (15 marks)
   (ii) Why is this your favourite section? Explain your answer with reference to the novel or short story you have chosen.   (15 marks)

(2009, Paper 2, Section 3, Fiction)

8 Spelling

Many students lose marks because of poor spelling. You can improve your overall grade by learning to spell correctly. Examine the list of commonly misspelled words below. Learn to spell each word correctly and check its meaning in a dictionary.

Commonly misspelled words

absolutely
accept
accidentally
achieve
across
address
although
always
anxious
apologise
appearance
argument
around
arrange
ascend
association
awful
awkward
background
beautiful
because
beginning
believe
benefit
between
bicycle
biscuit
breathe
brilliant
brought
business
category
caught
certain
character
choose
clothes
college
coming

committed
completely
concentrate
conscious
courageous
criticism
deceive
decision
definitely
descend
describe
desperate
development
different
disappear
disappointing
disaster
discuss
disease
doesn't
dropped
ecstasy
efficient
embarrassment
emergency
emphasise
enough
equipment
essential
every
exaggerate
excellent
excitement
exhausted
experience
extremely
fascinating
fierce
foreign

friends
fulfilled
government
grateful
guarantee
guard
happened
happiness
haven't
hear
height
heroes
hospital
humour
hypocrisy
illustrate
imagination
immediately
important
independent
influence
intelligence
interesting
irrelevant
knew
knight
knowledge
laugh
leave
leisure
library
licence (noun)
license (verb)
light
literature
loneliness
lonely
loose
magazine

maintenance	present	sometimes
making	privilege	sound
marriage	purpose	started
meant	queue	still
medicine	read	stopped
might	realise	straight
minutes	really	strategy
morning	receipt	success
mysterious	received	surprise
necessary	recognise	sympathy
nervous	recommend	thought
night	reference	together
nothing	reign	tragedy
nuisance	relief	tragic
occasion	religion	tranquil
occurred	repetition	truly
office	responsible	unconscious
once	restaurant	unnecessary
only	rhyme	until
opinion	rhythm	using
organise	ridiculous	usually
original	right	valuable
panicked	schedule	vengeance
parallel	scene	vicious
parliament	science	view
particularly	secretary	village
permanent	sense	weird
physical	separate	which
pleasant	should	while
please	similar	whole
poem	since	whose
possession	sincerely	would
practice (noun)	skilful	write
practise (verb)	solemn	
prejudice	something	

Easily confused words

The list of words below includes **homophones**: words that sound the same but have different meanings. Other easily confused words are also given. Consider how each word could be used incorrectly, e.g. **I would of** should be **I would have**. Learn how to spell each word in the list. Check its meaning in a dictionary. Then use it **correctly** in a sentence.

allowed	aloud	here	hear
bear	bare	higher	hire
fare	fair	hole	whole
for	four	hour	our
groan	grown	idol	idle

its	it's		thought	taught	
lone	loan		through	threw	
of	off		to	two	too
one	won		vain	vein	
pain	pane		warn	worn	
past	passed		waste	waist	
piece	peace		weak	week	
plane	plain		weather	whether	
purpose	propose		we're	were	
quiet	quite		wear	where	
sight	site		weight	wait	
steel	steal		whose	who's	
tail	tale		write	right	
their	there	they're	your	you're	

Acknowledgments

For permission to reproduce copyright material the publishers gratefully acknowledge the following:

'Darling Don't do that' by Tim Dowling reprinted by permission of A P Watt Ltd on behalf of Tim Dowling. Extract from 'A Swim for the Soul' by Róisín Ingle, 'Shhhhhhhhhh!' by Hugh Linehan, 'Slumdog Millionaire' film review by Michael Dwyer and '"Gift Grub" radio team mark 10-year anniversary of dishing out the satire' by Ronan McGreevy reprinted by permission of *The Irish Times*. Extract from *Singing for Mrs Pettigrew: A Storymaker's Journey* by Michael Morpurgo reprinted by permission of the author and David Higham Associates. *In Patagonia* by Bruce Chatwin, published by Jonathan Cape. Used by permission of The Random House Group Ltd. Extract from *Pictures in my Head* by Gabriel Byrne reprinted by kind permission of the author and the Red Letter Film Agency Ltd. *Snot's Green Sea* by Frances Cotter reprinted by permission of the author. 'My Pet Hates' by Rebecca Smith reprinted by permission of the author. *Extract from Adrian Mole and the Weapons of Mass Destruction by Sue Townsend*, London. Text copyright © Sue Townsend, 2004. Reproduced by permission of Penguin Books Ltd. Review of 'Endymion Spring' by Mary Shine Thompson reprinted by permission of *the Irish Independent*. 'Laboratory Rules for Pupils' reprinted by permission of *http://chemistry.slss.ie*. 'Brightest star goes out in the City of Angels' by Mark Hilliard from the Sunday Tribune of June 28 2009 and 'Watching Walls' by Mary O'Gorman reprinted by permission of the *Sunday Tribune*. 'Henry's £1bn cash in hand' by Nick Parker Copyright © *The Sun* 20th November 2009 / nisyndication.com reprinted by permission of *The Sun*. 'ITV1 dominates list of 2009's most-watched TV shows' by Tara Conlan reprinted by permission of The Guardian. Copyright © Guardian News & Media Ltd 2009 *Amphibians* first published in 1992 by Josef Weinberger Ltd (pka Warner/Chappell Plays Ltd.). Copyright © 1992 by Billy Roche. Reprinted by permission of Josef Weinberger Ltd. Extract from the play *Private Peaceful* adaption © Simon Reade 2004, based on the novel by Michael Morpurgo 'Private Peaceful' and other adaptions. Reprinted by permission of Oberon Books Ltd. 'Born Yesterday' and 'Coming' by Philip Larkin reprinted by permission of Marvell Press. 'In Memory of George Best' by Dermot Bolger reprinted by permission of A P Watt Ltd on behalf of Dermot Bolger. 'Fireworks' by James Reeves © James Reeves from *Complete Poems for Children* (FaberFinds). Reprinted by permission of the James Reeves Estate. Anthology available at www.faber.co.uk/faberfinds. 'Miracle on St David's Day' by Gillian Clarke, 2006, reprinted by permission of Carcanet Press Ltd. Louis Simpson 'Carentan O Carentan' from *A Dream of Governers* © 1959 by Louis Simpson and reprinted by permission of Wesleyan University Press. 'Leaning into the Afternoons' from *Selected Poems* by Pablo Neruda, translated by W.S. Merwin and published by Jonathan Cape. Reprinted by permission of The Random House Group Ltd. 'Pike' by Ted Hughes reprinted by permission of the author and Faber and Faber Ltd. 'Blessing' by Imtiaz Dharker from *Postcards from god* (Bloodaxe Books, 1997), reprinted by permission of Bloodaxe Books. 'Bog Child' by Siobhan Dowd, published by David Fickling Books. Reprinted by permission of The Random House Group Ltd. 'The Dragon Ring of Connla' from *Enchanted Irish Tales* by Patricia Lynch. Copyright © Estate of Patricia Lynch. Reprinted by kind permission of Mercier Press Ltd., Cork. *The Ring* by Bryan MacMahon reprinted by permission of A P Watt Ltd on behalf of Bryan MacMahon. *Circle of Friends* by Maeve Binchey, published by Century. Reprinted by permission of the Random House Group Ltd. Extract from *Point Blanc* by Anthony Horovitz, text © Anthony Horowitz. Trademarks Alex Rider™, Boy with torch Logo™©2010 Stormbreaker Productions Ltd. Reproduced by permission of Walker Books Ltd, London SE11 5HJ. www.walker.co.uk. Extract from *White Lies* by Mark O'Sullivan, published by Little Island Press, 2010. Reprinted by kind permission of Mark O'Sullivan.

The publishers have made every effort to trace copyright holders, but if they have inadvertently overlooked any they will be pleased to make the necessary arrangements at the first opportunity.